"This book does not coach a person with 'evang..... ..... will open your eyes to a world of wonder, a real world, in which there are as many witnesses as there are Christians, and there are as many approaches to the lost as there are believers. The game is on, and everyone can play!"
ENRIQUE SANTIS, GENERAL MANAGER, VINEYARD MUSIC LATIN, ANAHEIM, CALIFORNIA

"Through a fresh, invigorating reading of the gospel, and through moving stories about real people seeking and finding, John Teter brings us a fresh, invigorating love of Jesus, which then 'launches' us into his love for people."
DARRELL W. JOHNSON, ASSOCIATE PROFESSOR OF PASTORAL THEOLOGY, REGENT COLLEGE, VANCOUVER, BRITISH COLUMBIA

"John Teter has written an engaging, inspiring and biblical book that repeatedly caused me to interrupt my reading with a simple prayer: 'God use me to get your Word out.' I'm excited about using this book with young leaders to help them live out the 'why' of Christian leadership—the Great Commission."
STEVE MOORE, LEADERSHIP COACH AND CONSULTANT, TOP FLIGHT LEADERSHIP

"As someone who has known and served with John for several years, I can honestly say that Teter lives what he writes. I clearly felt God prodding me to 'get the Word out' more than I typically do, but this came more as a result of John's unique blend of exposition, humor and candor than being made to feel guilty. This book is both accessible and profound—just like the gospel is!"
KEN FONG, SENIOR PASTOR, EVERGREEN BAPTIST CHURCH OF LOS ANGELES, AND AUTHOR OF SECURE IN GOD'S EMBRACE

"Lives are transformed by the Word and our daily commitment to be witnesses. John helps us engage our commitment to be witnesses of the good news in Jesus. Our witness is based on being shaped by the Word and led by the Spirit as we follow Jesus into our world. This book is a must-read for engaging our diverse postmodern world."
GERI RODMAN, PRESIDENT, INTERVARSITY CHRISTIAN FELLOWSHIP OF CANADA

"John's infectious love for Jesus, his skilled treatment of Scripture and his burning passion to see people empowered to reach the lost make this book a must-read for anyone who has ever wanted to lead friends and loved ones to Christ but doubted they had the right stuff. John convincingly proves that believers not only have the right stuff, but the right stuff will become sweeter as we share our faith with those who need it the most.

REV. ALEXANDER GEE JR., PASTOR, COMMUNITY LEADER, LECTURER, AUTHOR

"*Get the Word Out* pulsates with a passion to share the joy of knowing Jesus. With enthusiasm, keen insights, practicality, relevance and clarity, John Teter sings the music of one who has fallen in love with Jesus."

DAVE GIBBONS, LEAD PASTOR OF NEWSONG CHURCH, AND BOARD MEMBER, WORLD VISION UNITED STATES

"With compelling and sometimes hilarious honesty, John reveals the true hero in witness—Jesus Christ. His immersion into and subsequent truth-challenges from the Gospel of John provide a fresh invitation to embrace transformation and partner in kingdom work."

SHELLEY TREBESCH, PH.D.

GET THE WORD OUT

How God Shapes
and Sends His Witnesses

JOHN TETER

InterVarsity Press
Downers Grove, Illinois

InterVarsity Press
P.O. Box 1400, Downers Grove, IL 60515-1426
World Wide Web: www.ivpress.com
E-mail: mail@ivpress.com

InterVarsity Press® is the book-publishing division of InterVarsity Christian Fellowship/USA®, a student movement active on campus at hundreds of universities, colleges and schools of nursing in the United States of America, and a member movement of the International Fellowship of Evangelical Students. For information about local and regional activities, write Public Relations Dept., InterVarsity Christian Fellowship/USA, 6400 Schroeder Rd., P.O. Box 7895, Madison, WI 53707-7895, or visit the IVCF website at <www.ivcf.org>.

Scripture quotations, unless otherwise noted, are from the New Revised Standard Version of the Bible, copyright 1989 by the Division of Christian Education of the National Council of the Churches of Christ in the USA. Used by permission. All rights reserved.

Design: Cindy Kiple

Images: Digital Vision/Getty Images

The logo for Get the Word Out Ministries (pp. 12, 168) provided by Get the Word Out Ministries. The diagram on page 12 was designed by Matt J. Smith.

ISBN 0-8308-2365-4

Printed in the United States of America ∞

Library of Congress Cataloging-in-Publication Data

Teter, John, 1970-
 Get the word out: how God shapes and sends his witnesses / John Teter.
    p. cm.
Includes bibliographical references.
 ISBN 0-8308-2365-4 (pbk.: alk. paper)
 1. Evangelistic work. I. Title
 BV3790.T47 2003
 269'.2—dc21

                                                          2003010908

P 17 16 15 14 13 12 11 10 9 8 7 6 5 4 3 2 1

Y 15 14 13 12 11 10 09 08 07 06 05 04 03

For my wonderful wife,

Rebecca Megumi Teter.

You are Jesus' good wine to me.

Contents

Foreword by J. Robert Clinton 9

Introduction 13

1. JESUS, LOVER OF MY SOUL 23

2. WHO WILL GIVE YOU PROPS? 36

3. WITNESS TO WORSHIP 52

4. SEEKERS OR SNACKERS? 69

5. SENT BY GOD 86

6. FILLED WITH THE SPIRIT 103

7. FOLLOWED BY JESUS 121

Growth Project 1:
   Blisters or Calluses? How Witnesses Grow 137

Growth Project 2:
   Becoming a GIG Leader 151

Acknowledgments 166

Contact Information 168

FOREWORD

In his introduction to this book, John Teter dares to include the following prayer:

> It is my prayer that this book will help you begin your own Word-based evangelism ministry.

Why? Because he fervently believes that what he says in this book can do just that. But there is a catch. He goes on to say, "If you are willing to commit to God to be his witness, he will be faithful to shape and lead you." John Teter can pray that prayer and make that claim because he has seen it happen on college campuses.

John was a student of mine several years ago in a course called "Lifelong Development." As I read his personal case study, I was impressed with who God was shaping John to be. I saw that John had a heart to study God's Word and allow it to permeate his own thinking. In addition, I knew he was doing some experimenting with evangelism on campuses—both residential and community colleges. He had become aware that a new movement was in the making. A new student population was emerging—one that was open to exploring the gospel. What John needed was some way of reaching them.

Out of his heart for studying the Word and his desire to communicate it evangelistically on campuses, John developed exploratory Bible study groups based on a long tradition within InterVarsity of investigative Bible discussions. InterVarsity called these studies GIGs—Groups Investigating God. As a result of these studies, John began to see people coming to Christ—lives changed. He knew he was on to something. So he began to pass on what he was learning to others.

About two years ago he came to me with a question: "I want to share with others what I have been learning about evangelism on campuses. The Gospel of John is a core book for me, and I want to write a book for InterVarsity Press on evangelism using the communication principles embedded in that great book. Would you mentor me in my study of John's Gospel?"

So we set out on a study project. For over a year John diligently studied the Gospel of John, observing the breakthrough communication principles in Jesus' ministry. He intuitively knew that those communication principles were at the heart of his GIGs approach.

Get the Word Out is the result of that foundational time in the Gospel of John. The ideas from John's Gospel are interwoven throughout the book. John is not kidding when he uses the phrase "Word-based evangelism."

John's experiment continues to grow. Others have caught the dynamics of GIGs as he communicates them in his inspirational sermons, personally disciples others in the approach and then leads InterVarsity campus workers and students in training seminars and workshops.

This book is another means for John to inspire even more people to challenge others to explore the claims of Jesus. The highlights of the book include

- a strong biblical base—it is filled with material from John's Gospel (this book is worth its price just for the insights into John's Gospel)

- dynamic communication principles—ideas that can be transferred to anyone's ministry

- illustrations from actual experiences on campus—the kind that inspire yet teach (the illustrations alone make the book worthwhile)

- an author who models what he is teaching to others and is transparent—both successes and failures punch home his emphases
- pithy summaries with a personal growth challenge at the conclusion of each chapter

So become an answer to John Teter's prayer. Read this book. Be inspired to start your own Word-based evangelism ministry. See lives transformed. And like John Teter, pass on to others what you learn.

Dr. J. Robert (Bobby) Clinton
Professor of Leadership
School of World Mission
Fuller Theological Seminary

BEARING FRUIT
FOR ETERNAL LIFE

4. Seekers or Snackers?

7. Followed by Jesus

5. Sent by God

6. Filled with the Spirit

3. Witness to Worship

Growth Project: Blisters or Callouses?

Growth Project: Becoming a GIG Leader

2. Who Will Give You Props?

1. Jesus, Lover of My Soul

INTRODUCTION

Follow me, and I will make you fish for people.

JESUS OF NAZARETH

When I was in high school, I never dreamed evangelism would be in my future. God wasn't even on my screen, let alone telling other people about him. I was too busy with going to detention, skipping class for the beach and partying like a rock star. In fact, if people who knew me in my high school days stumble upon this book, they will certainly assume it was written by someone else who just happens to have my name. I'm not kidding.

Growing up, church was not a part of my family experience. I can remember going to church exactly twice in my first ten years. In junior high I was involved in church for one year and had a positive experience. But by the time high school rolled around, I couldn't stand being around Christians. I went out of my way to avoid them. Some of it was Christian culture, some of it was high school culture, but the impressions were powerful and stayed with me.

The Christians always seemed to have their religious frowns cast in my direction. I even received a five-page handwritten letter from an entire small group that warned me to repent of my partying ways because God was going to judge me and hell was certainly in my near future. I wish they hadn't written that letter. I wish instead that they would have asked me about the family tragedy that had left a hole in my heart. That was what I was trying to fill with all of the partying. After that letter, I went out of my way to get further out of the Christians' way.

But here I am writing a book on evangelism. God has done a mighty work in my life. In his sovereign love and wisdom, he gave me the foundation of an unbelieving past so that I would understand non-Christians. I have learned the most about evangelism from my own conversion experience. My soul warms every time I read about Paul in Acts testifying three separate times about his own conversion. Like Paul's, my soul burns brightly with thanksgiving to God for his grace. I echo the words of the psalmist who said, "The boundary lines have fallen for me in pleasant places" (Psalm 16:6). I have tried to understand the experience of conversion God gave to me so that I can help others in their own conversion experience. I have been on the receiving end of insensitive and irrelevant witness, but I have also experienced outstanding relational evangelism. That was how God rescued my soul my first year at college. I am eager to share what I have learned.

Evangelism is not easy. It is hard to lead our family and friends to live under the love and leadership of an invisible God. It is a challenge to articulate our faith and answer deep spiritual questions in a world that is hostile to the gospel. And it certainly is a great challenge to teach the Bible to people who think King David was a rapper from the East Coast. Yes, our challenges are large. But Jesus is more committed to making us people who get his word out than we are.

Jesus told the fishermen, his first followers, that he would make them fish for people. Evangelism is the promise in his call for commitment. And Jesus takes his promises seriously. He is the Great Trainer who is committed to developing evangelists. He took Peter from fishing in Galilee to leading thousands to faith in Jerusalem. Peter's destiny was to become a fisher of people. And so is ours. But it didn't happen overnight and it didn't happen without some failures along the way.

EVANGELISM AND .400 HITTERS

The highs of being a witness are incredible. And the lows are devastating. Witness is a call that promises failure and disappointment. If we expect that reality from the beginning, however, we won't be so fragile when rejection hits us like a ton of bricks. Maybe it will feel like only half a ton of bricks.

As I reflect on my own development as a witness, I think of the game of baseball. From the time I could walk, I have loved the Los Angeles Dodgers and major league baseball. Ted Williams, who played for the Boston Red Sox, is recognized as possibly the greatest hitter in the history of baseball. He was the last player to hit over .400. The game has been played for over fifty years since Williams's magical year, and no one has been able to match his feat.

The fact that .400 is the most celebrated feat for a hitter should tell us something about baseball. The game's best hitter, in the most outstanding year of his career, failed to hit safely six times out of ten. That means he walked back to the dugout, failing to reach base safely, more times than he got a hit. Yet I imagine Ted Williams held his head high when he went back to the bench. He had learned experientially that baseball is a difficult game. He didn't expect to reach base every at bat.

In the same way, living as Jesus' witness in this world requires proper perspective. We will make many mistakes. It may take years and years of labor before we become an effective witness. That was the case for me. I believe I have experienced growth as a witness because of the simple fact that I never gave up. I always walk to the proverbial dugout with my head held high, knowing that making an out is part of the witness experience. It was years and years before I saw my personal witness change anyone's life. It was through great humiliation and personal shame that I learned to be a teacher of Jesus' Word. It was because of many awkward and painful conversations that I have learned how to build trust and challenge my non-Christian friends. I have made many outs. But I have never given up.

During my first years of evangelism, my average was below .100. If it were baseball, I would likely have been sent down to the minor leagues. But Jesus taught me great lessons through failure and is fulfilling his promise to me to make me a fisher of people. He will do the same for you.

All of us can become effective witnesses if we do not give up. But we must realize from the outset that there are no shortcuts. I recently had an experience in which God reminded me of the need for good old-fashioned perseverance.

PERSEVERANCE AND DEDICATION

I am a full-time campus pastor with InterVarsity Christian Fellowship. One day I was working on my laptop computer in the campus library when I locked my laptop to the chair I was sitting in. While I was messing around with this new lock, I accidentally changed the combination to a number I didn't know. At first I thought it was amusing. But then I realized I had no way to remove my computer from the chair. I began to panic when I looked at my watch and realized I needed to preach a sermon in one hour.

Reviewing my sermon notes and praying for the worship time ahead was suddenly no longer an option. For the next hour, I struggled to open the lock. I prayed to God and even asked him to tell me the numbers. That didn't work. I tried to pry the lock open. That failed. As the worship service drew near, I had no other choice but to take the chair with me. I picked it up and walked the chair right out the front door of the library with the laptop locked to the leg. The student librarian looked up in a moment of confusion as I whisked by, but before she could speak, I was out the door.

I ended up bringing the chair home with me that night. I didn't know what else to do. I awoke early the next morning for a meeting and left the computer and chair at home. I explained to my wife, Becky, what had happened the night before. She got a good laugh out of this one.

The next day I was at a meeting and called Becky at lunch. She had opened the lock! I was thrilled. I asked her how she did it. She said that she started at oooo and kept increasing the four-digit combination one number at a time, trying to open the lock at each turn. It finally clicked open at o386. The only way she could free the computer from the chair leg was by turning the lock 386 times. At least the new combo wasn't 9998. I thanked her profusely. I had regained my computer from the chair, which I returned to the library the next day. (Campus ministers shouldn't steal furniture from the campus library.)

From the computer lock experience, I learned a lesson about life and evangelism. There are no shortcuts to freedom. If we are to become witnesses, we must learn our lessons in Jesus' school of witness development. We all wish we could pray one prayer and then suddenly become modern-day John the Baptists. While some recent converts might experience God's kingdom in this way, most of us will not. The excitement of conversion occurs only because of the daily commitment to being a witness. God will not allow us to shortchange the process of him shaping and sending us for witness.

Persevering, remaining dedicated to the "lock turning" fundamentals of being an evangelist, is hard work. That should be fine with us, though, because our witness is all about the people we love. It is all about our family, our friends, our coworkers, the people at the grocery store, our new neighbors who just moved in. We won't get publicity for leading them to faith, but we will have the thrill of our life in seeing God move.

Personal witnesses aren't flashy. We are faithful. Our lives are to be marked by patient suffering as we walk with sinners through their process of conversion. The suffering will be manifest, for example, with late-night phone calls when the non-Christians we love call us as their life is falling apart. And our hearts will be set apart with thanksgiving because the suffering is worth it. Personal witness is all about showing up with a good attitude. If we do not give up but rather let God grow us to engage our friends and teach them the Bible, we can all become effective witnesses.

GIGS LOS ANGELES
EVANGELISM TRAINING

This book was birthed from an evangelism training program I created for the InterVarsity Christian Fellowship campus work in Los Angeles. Forty students and staff committed to the year-long training program. The growth was encouraging. People who were obviously gifted and wired for evangelism, and those who weren't, became effective witnesses.

My vision was to inspire and train people to lead their unchurched friends into understanding and responding to the Bible. These studies are called GIGs, an acronym for "Groups Investigating God." GIGs are small-group Bible studies for non-Christians. They are effective because they help non-Christians see Jesus in his Word without all the trappings people associate with religion. They have also proven effective in helping non-Christians move forward in their process of conversion to genuine discipleship. I became a Christian through a GIG in 1992. And I have been leading seeker Bible studies ever since.

The staff and students grew tremendously that year in learning to lead their own GIG ministries. They took great strides in communicating with non-Christians. They prayed with greater urgency and effectiveness and saw God move in response to their intercession. They became better teachers of God's Word and were surprised at how eager non-Christians are to study the Word. They became people who believed God wanted to use them to reach their friends.

Here is a testimony from John Negrete, one of the students who developed into a witness:

I have never prayed for God to let me lead somebody into the kingdom until I was challenged by the training program to lead at least one person into the kingdom by the end of the academic school year. It was one of the lofty goals of our group. And I think that this has been one of the greatest lessons I've taken away from the meetings. No challenge is too impossible or too crazy for God. And I think that's how I've changed the most as an evangelist, realizing that it is possible for me. Not just other people. Not just Becky Pippert. But me.

In my GIG I was teaching the Bible to a Jewish woman who was checking Jesus out. I boldly invited her to an evangelistic conference for non-Christians in GIG studies. I told her that it would be good for her. She thought about it and decided to go. In that invitation I saw that what I was learning was true. We have a lot more room and trust with our friends who are interested in Jesus than we think. We can challenge them and be bold without having to be afraid they won't like us anymore or will stop coming to the GIG.

The weekend of the conference I really pushed my self-imposed limits on what I could say to her. Jesus was speaking to her in real ways, and I helped her interpret what he was saying to her. I spoke to her with conviction, knowing I was sent to her by God. This Jewish woman, who had come to seven GIG studies, decided to follow Jesus that weekend and is now growing in her faith. It has been an incredible gift to be the one who led her into Jesus' kingdom. God answered my prayer for the year that I might personally lead someone to Jesus.

This experience was tailored to strengthen my faith and boldness. I saw God come through for me, and my trust in his voice skyrocketed that day. I would never have taken that risk if I hadn't been challenged. I've never even conceived of doing something like that. I've only heard stories. And now I have my own stories. There have been more since then.

Witnesses are developed. Jesus promises that to those he calls. The question is whether we are willing to commit to a development process that offers no shortcuts. The call before us is profoundly humbling, and it promises rejection and failure. But when we compare the personal costs and sacrifices we will endure to the immeasurable joy that is offered to the witness, how can we pass up such a great offer from Jesus?

WHO IS THIS BOOK FOR?

For the past two years, I have spent my time planting new urban campus ministries for InterVarsity in Los Angeles. My job requires crosscultural evangelism, crosscultural evangelism and more crosscultural evangelism. Hearing that, you may be jealous of how I get to spend my time. If so, this book is for you. Others of you, however, might prefer to be tortured and killed rather than sign off on that job description. If so, this book is also for you. You don't have to be the apostle Paul to lead your friends and family to Jesus; you just have to be open to God's shaping power to make you a witness. We can all do that.

Each chapter in the book has biblical foundations from John's Gospel. From September 1998 to September 2000, I studied the Fourth Gospel intensively. I began studying the Fourth Gospel because I was drawn to the imagery of water, bread and light. But as I went deeper, I discovered that John's Gospel paints a picture of God's supreme victory in evangelism and teaches us how God develops his evangelists. I want to share that picture with you.

Let me give you an idea of what to expect in the chapters that lie ahead. The first three chapters are all about getting the Word deep into us. It must be in us before we get it out. We will focus on what it means to belong to Jesus and enjoy an intimate relationship with him. We will also spotlight how the praise of other people proves anathema to our leading our friends to faith. We will then take a look at what it means that witnessing is good for us, the witness. The command to witness is not meant just to bless the world; it is meant to bless us as well. Chapter four is the hinge that connects the Word in us to the world. We have much to learn from how Jesus loved and handled the world. The final three chapters draw our attention to God's commitment to his witnesses as we win the world through witness. God is not distant in any dimension of our evangelism experience. He goes before us, he is behind us and he is even inside of us. We are offered endless intimacy and resources as we get the Word out—with God, never apart from him. We are not alone.

The book concludes with two growth projects. The first examines the practical steps to becoming a witness. If we are to become witnesses who grow over the course of a lifetime, we will need guiding principles and values to direct us into that growth. The second growth project details how you can start your own GIG ministry. After all, it is through hearing *and* doing the Word of God that we grow.

WHAT THIS BOOK IS AND ISN'T

This book is not a training manual. I believe that training conferences and seminar workshops are the best venues for training. This book is meant to inform, inspire and motivate you to take the next step as a witness. That step will be different depending on who we are and what kind of experience we have as witnesses. If you are new to evangelism, it is my prayer that this book will help you begin your own Word-based evangelism ministry. If you have been a witness for many years, I pray this book will encourage you to go deeper with Jesus and experience the joy of bearing an ever-increasing amount of fruit. And if you are an evangelism leader, I pray this book will assist you as you lead the people of God into witness in a rapidly changing world.

I have included stories of people who have recently become followers of Jesus. Where appropriate, I have changed the names of the people involved. I hope these testimonies of God's work encourage

you. I have tried to give full accounts of conversations, where necessary, to help you get a feel for my communication style with non-
Christians. I find it helpful to observe others and how they communicate the gospel. I hope that my stories, both the failures and the vic-
tories, will help you in your own evangelism development.

As you read the stories of how God moved, please remember that
my greatest trait as a witness is the refusal to give up. Over the past
ten years, I have had many reasons to stop sharing my faith with my
friends. I have hit many walls that appeared too high to climb. But
God has always been faithful to help me ask the right questions and
send me mentors to help me learn and help me grow. Some of those
mentors ministered with me. Others I learned from through their
writings. If you are willing to commit to being Christ's witness, he
will be faithful to shape and send you.

Please join me as together we become more fruitful and joyful witnesses. But don't believe that God develops us as his witnesses just
because I said so. It is Jesus who calls us. Your non-Christian friends
and family will be eternally grateful if you accept his call. May the
Holy Spirit use this book to inspire and motivate us all to become
burning, shining lamps in this dark and dying world. Amen.

ONE

JESUS, LOVER OF MY SOUL

You must be the change you wish to see in the world.

MOHANDAS K. GANDHI

It's all about a spiritual renewal.
It's all about feeling born again,
not necessarily believing in a logical term.

KIRK FRANKLIN

God is not looking for burned-out, guilt-ridden evangelists to change the world. There are enough of those folks doing their thing in the world. Instead God is looking for people who are madly in love with his Son, experience him as the best joy in all the world and therefore cannot contain their joy in God. That is what it means to be sent as a witness.

We are shaped by God's love before we are sent. The order is important. Just as most marriage relationships don't happen by chance, so it is in our spiritual love affair with Jesus. God initiates with us. We love God because God first loved us (1 John 4:19). That is great news!

Before God would have us launch forth into a hostile world to introduce his love to sinners, he would have us be people who are first consumed with that same love. He would have us give to others what we ourselves have experienced. His design for us is that we would minister to the world as we draw from the overflowing resources of his love.

TRANSFORMING LOVE

When we are in love, life becomes strangely wonderful. The food tastes better, sleep suddenly becomes optional, and ten-minute phone calls morph into four-hour talk marathons. And the desire to declare our love may cause us to make elaborate plans to please the one we love.

As I thought about proposing to my wife, I wanted to do something to make it special so that Becky would know how much I loved her. When she signed up for a Christian community development conference in Chicago, I decided to fly to Chicago and surprise her there.

I asked for help from my friend Pastor Alex Gee—a Midwesterner and a romantic. It turned out that he was going to be in Chicago leading a seminar at the same conference Becky was attending. We decided that he would invite Becky to a dinner to meet his church-planting mentors. Alex stressed how special his mentors were to ensure that Becky would arrive in her nicest outfit. (Of course, this invitation was just a set-up to meet me.) Meanwhile, I reserved a table at the Signature Room in the John Hancock Center. It is located ninety-five stories above downtown Chicago. The entire restaurant is enclosed in glass, and on a clear night the experience is like dining in a cloud.

The week before I proposed, I was busy with preparations. My mom gave me the diamond that my father had given to her when they married. They were married twenty-seven years before my father's untimely death in a single-passenger plane accident. The ring was perfect. The modest but stunning diamond floated above the delicate gold band. Mom also gave me a wonderful letter she had written to welcome Becky into our family.

From the moment I left my mom's house until the moment I met Becky in Chicago, I kept the ring in my pocket. I preached at a conference with the ring in my pocket. I ran errands at a mall with the ring in my pocket. I got a haircut with the ring in my pocket. I picked out my engagement shirt and tie with the ring in my pocket. I went to church with the ring in my pocket. I just couldn't let the ring go. It possessed greater powers over me than Tolkien's ring. This ring was purchased and passed on for love. It symbolized the love of my parents. And now it captured the love that would fill the new life Jesus had ahead for Becky and me.

On the morning of November 17 I boarded a plane for Chicago. I hadn't slept at all the night before. During the flight, I read my Bible, tried to record my rapidly swirling thoughts in my journal and practiced over and over again the words I would say to Becky. After I felt confident and practiced up, I told my neighbor all about Becky and my mission of love. And I made sure to show him the ring that I still had in my pocket.

I finally arrived at the restaurant on the ninety-fifth floor. The manager directed Becky to the bar where she was (supposedly) to wait for Alex. Ten minutes later the general manager gave her a package that contained a live cell phone, and I called her on that phone. I told her I was in L.A. eating dinner with my mom, and we chatted for about ten minutes. As we prepared to say goodbye, I told her that I had another surprise for her at the front desk.

When I saw Becky walking down the stairs, my heart leaped into my throat. Somehow I managed to meet her at the bottom. That night we were engaged.

We become different because of the people we spend our days with. We grow together and in new dimensions when we are in love. For example, while I used to never have much of an interest in food, I now have a new zeal to learn about food and spend time in the kitchen. That is the influence of Becky. On another level, my heart, mind and ministry philosophy have been transformed because of my life with Becky. In a few short years, God has led me to become an urban minister on a commuter-college campus. Through my life with Becky he has strengthened the value I place on reconciliation, justice and investing in the lives of youth. And God has given me a new confidence, a new boldness and a new joy in life because of Becky as a tangible reminder that I am loved.

How much more powerful is the transformation when the person who loves on us is not another human but God himself? As we live day to day with Jesus, we become more like him. That is the hope of the apostle Paul, who wrote that God's design is to change us from glory to glory (2 Corinthians 3:18). When we are filled with his love, we will offer that same love to others.

THE WOMAN AT THE WELL

The biblical story of the woman at the well is an incredible example of being chosen in love and embodying that message of love in a hostile world.

[Jesus] had to go through Samaria. So he came to a Samaritan city called Sychar, near the plot of ground that Jacob had given to his son Joseph. Jacob's well was there, and Jesus, tired out by his journey, was sitting by the well. It was about noon.

A Samaritan woman came to draw water, and Jesus said to her, "Give me a drink." (His disciples had gone to the city to buy food.) The Samaritan woman said to him, "How is it that you, a Jew, ask a drink of me, a woman of Samaria?" (Jews do not share things in common with Samaritans.) Jesus answered her, "If you knew the gift of God, and who it is that is saying to you, 'Give me a drink,' you would have asked him, and he would have given you living water." The woman said to him, "Sir, you have no bucket, and the well is deep. Where do you get that living water? Are you greater than our ancestor Jacob, who gave us the well, and with his sons and his flocks drank from it?" Jesus said to her, "Everyone who drinks of this water will be thirsty again, but those who drink of the water that I will give them will never be thirsty. The water that I will give will become in them a spring of water gushing up to eternal life." The woman said to him, "Sir, give me this water, so that I may never be thirsty or have to keep coming here to draw water."

Jesus said to her, "Go, call your husband, and come back." The woman answered him, "I have no husband." Jesus said to her, "You are right in saying, 'I have no husband'; for you have had five husbands, and the one you have now is not your husband. What you have said is true!" . . . The woman said to him, "I know that Messiah is coming" (who is called Christ). "When he comes, he will proclaim all things to us." Jesus said to her, "I am he, the one who is speaking to you."

Just then his disciples came. They were astonished that he was speaking with a woman, but no one said, "What do you want?" or, "Why are you speaking with her?" Then the woman left her water jar and went back to the city. She said to the people, "Come and see a man who told me everything I have ever done! He cannot be the Messiah, can he?" They left the city and were on their way to him. (John 4:4-18, 25-30)

This story contains many details that are useful for modern-day witnesses to note. One thing not to miss is how the woman at the well left her jar behind as she went to reach out to her Samaritan city.

The first-century practice of drawing water was a grueling task that women would do together at either sunrise or sunset to avoid the heat. Whether by her choice or by insistence from the members of the community, this woman went alone in the heat of noon to draw water. The reason for her isolation becomes clear when we learn that she had been married five times and was now living with a sixth man. Gossip, judgment and exclusion are as old as dirt.

The abandoned water jar offers a symbolic framework of the woman's life. I imagine every day she would set out to try to quench her thirst and that of her home. This must have been a lonely experience for her. The weight of her jar was a burden she would have to carry daily. Her physical thirst likely reminded her of her relational thirst. The water that would leak from the cracks in the jar resembled the love that always seemed to slip through her grasp. Why were the men in her life so wishy-washy? How could they be so cruel to her? How could they reject her so easily and so often? Her life, like the jar, was weathered and cracked from her suffering, regret and toil.

When the woman at the well dropped her water jar to run to the city, she was not merely leaving something behind in haste. She had found liberation and life in the transforming love of God. The woman who had been thirsty her whole life had now become the well that the rest of her thirsty city would drink from. As Darrell Johnson puts it, "The woman at the well became a well." Transformation abounds where love explodes.

SIGNS OF LOVE

John 4 is a love story. And in this story we find four clues embedded in Jewish culture and the Old Testament about the nature of God's love. These highlights help us understand what happened at the well that day.

1. *The well.* For John's first audience, Jesus' meeting the woman at Jacob's well would have set off bells. In fact, they would have sounded like wedding bells. The well was where many of the forefathers met their future wives. For example, Genesis 24 tells how Abraham's servant was sent out with instructions to find Isaac a wife. After calling on God for direction and blessing, the servant met Rebekah at the well. The well was also the location where both Jacob and Moses met their wives (Genesis 29:2; Exodus 2:15). So when John mentioned that Jesus met the woman at the well, his readers were aware that God had

a track record of bringing people together at a well for great purposes.

2. *"Give me a drink."* Jesus' first words were carefully crafted and must have caused the hearts of this Gospel's first hearers to skip a beat. "Give me a drink" was the exact phrase that Abraham's servant spoke to Rebekah as he was seeking to find the wife God had chosen for Isaac (Genesis 24:17). The servant asked God for a sign—namely that the woman whom God wanted as a wife for Isaac would respond to the servant's needs. Rebekah proved to be hospitable to Abraham's servant, even to the point of gathering water for the horses.

The New Testament proclaims that Jesus was the fulfillment of the great Old Testament hope that God, the great Bridegroom, would claim his bride, forever removing her shame and reproach. This was no mere servant sent to find a wife; this was the living God, sent by his Father to fulfill his great promise to be the Bridegroom to his people.

3. *Jeremiah's living water.* Jesus also repeated words spoken nearly six hundred years earlier by the prophet Jeremiah. Jeremiah 2, the prophet's first sermon, is a scathing indictment of Israel's unfaithfulness in her marriage to the living God. Jeremiah condemned Israel's addiction to other lovers, its constant hardness to God's love and the nation's choice to drink from a leaky and broken cistern. The prophet declared that the heavens were appalled at Israel's unfaithful behavior, and he condemned the nation for rejecting God's living water because they were full of holes (Jeremiah 2:13).

Jesus asked the woman if she would like to drink his water. He used the same words of Jeremiah to promise that his living water would bring satisfaction to her soul and healing to her life. Jesus did not condemn the woman for her unfaithfulness; he wanted her to learn to drink from a relationship that was not beneath her dignity.

4. *John the Baptist.* The last clue to the spiritual and relational dynamics in John 4 is found at the end of the previous chapter of John. There John the Baptist describes his identity in relationship to Jesus: "He who has the bride is the bridegroom. The friend of the bride-

groom, who stands and hears him, rejoices greatly at the bridegroom's voice. For this reason my joy has been fulfilled. He must
increase, but I must decrease" (John 3:29-30). John's role was similar
to that of the best man in today's Western weddings. At the end of
chapter 3 we are left with the question, who is the bride?

Jesus is the Bridegroom at the altar of God on his wedding day. He
is blameless, beaming and eager to receive his bride. John the Baptist, the best man, stands at his right hand. He is Jesus' most loyal
friend. The bride's anthem begins. The crowd stands up and looks to
the back of the church. The doors open . . . and then the chapter
abruptly ends. We scratch our heads. Who will walk down the aisle?
It is at this moment of drama that chapter 4 begins.

THE WEAK ARE CHOSEN FOR LOVE

Jesus committed himself to the woman at the well. We might be
tempted to ask why Jesus chose her. But we must remember that the
choice was not Jesus' doing. Jesus taught that he did only what he saw
the Father doing (John 5:19). Jesus' choosing the woman at the well
was his Father's idea. It was consistent with the nature of his choosing
love. God has always chosen the weak to humble the strong and glorify his name.

God chose Abram, a moon worshiper from Ur, to be the father
of many nations. He chose Jacob, the second son, and not Esau, to
be the namesake of his nation. God chose to be Israel's God because it was the smallest and weakest of all the nations. God chose
to exalt David, the little shepherd boy, not the other would-be kings
pegged for greatness. He did all this to bring glory to his name,
which gives ultimate worth to all peoples. And God opposes those
who scorn his name.

Likewise, as we learn in John's Gospel, Jesus did not choose the
great community leader, the brilliant theologian or the elite and suc-
cessful of society. He chose a person who was defined by rejection,

scarred from sin and living as an outcast. He didn't pick someone who had it all together. He committed himself to an emotional time bomb. If we are honest, you or I would probably admit to being uneasy about sharing a lunch with the woman at the well, let alone committing the rest of our lives to her. Yet Jesus embraced her loneliness, pain, addictions, patterns of sin and emotional fatigue.

The Father, full of confidence in his ability to transform people by his love, knows that human beings are not their brokenness. He knows that his love gives us all power to become children of God. Just as Jesus turned water into wine, so he chose to turn the woman at the well into a beautiful bride. Choosing the woman at the well was yet another magnificent display of God's tender love.

Why did Jesus choose to call out her sexual past? Not exactly the smoothest interaction in a shame-based culture, was it? Yet Jesus always did the right thing. So how was this the right thing for the woman?

The shadows in the woman's past only enhanced the glorious colors of Jesus' grace. It is good news—profoundly good news—that Jesus brought out all of her baggage before they began traveling together. He did not want the woman at the well to think that his commitment was predicated on her goodness. He wanted her to realize from the outset that he knew everything she had ever done. He brought out the skeletons in the closet before she could worry about them down the road.

We do not have to carry those burdens that weigh us down. With Jesus, nothing is too wonderful to be true. It is sinners like the Samaritan woman and you and me whom Jesus of Nazareth chooses to grow old with. He wants to have breakfast with us every morning. The offer of a relationship with Jesus seems too good to be true, yet it is true.

If our human relationships are built upon the foundations of authenticity and honesty, how much more true is that in our relationship with God? As people who long to be used by God as deliverers of the good news in this world, we must keep our relationship with God fresh and precious. We must always be honest with him. He is faithful, so it is safe to reveal to him our gaping needs. When we try to be people we are not, to impress God, we have missed the gospel. He loves on the weak and dotes on the needy.

A WELL FOR A THIRSTY WORLD

Witnesses are not called to make people become Christians. Witnesses point others to Jesus and introduce them to him. Then Jesus takes over. The woman at the well was filled with God's love and went to those who had cast her out. When she appeared with passion and confidence, her soul soaring because of love, the village was all ears. The entire city canceled their schedule and went out to spend two days with Jesus.

Isn't it interesting that Jesus gave the woman no command to go and share her faith? She was not sent in an official commissioning ceremony as were the disciples in John 20:20-22. She instinctively responded to the love of God given to her by giving it away to others, even the very people who drove her into outcast status. She had tasted the living water, and now it bubbled up within her to eternal life. This life flowed over onto her village. Such was not the case for the disciples.

In stark contrast to the woman, the disciples needed Jesus to spell out the nature of witness for them. He gave them a parable about the harvest, unlocked the process of evangelism, promised them that witness would be for their own joy and told them to lift their eyes because it was happening right before their eyes. They just didn't get it. At this stage of their development as witnesses, they were not desperate enough. To them the living water was nice, no doubt. But for the woman, Jesus' water was life or death. The woman at the well was won by the love of God; in her overflow, she won the city.

Our families, friends and cities need the same message. Our non-

Christian friends are starved for love and yearn for stability and wholeness but have no idea that Jesus waits for them at the altar. They think Jesus is critical of them, unemotional and unmoved by their spiritual plight. Jesus wants them to know that if he will commit to the woman at the well, he will commit to them. How many of our friends think Jesus embraces people with problems? If they are to hear this good news, they need to see it first in our lives.

I fear that the Jesus we reveal today is a Jesus who functions as a distant consultant to self-sufficient religious people. The Jesus our friends see helps us be faithful with our quiet times, helps us not swear when we get frustrated and helps us not cheat on taxes or tests. But they hardly ever see the Jesus who understands sexual addiction. They never get a glimpse of the Jesus who isn't afraid of eating disorders, violence, bitterness, broken families or any other manner of sin we find ourselves under. They just can't imagine a Jesus who gets deeply involved with messy, needy sinners. All of the images they have internalized depict Jesus as a shepherd who strokes his sheep with a glazed, whimsical look while he sings religious songs as if he were Ned Flanders from *The Simpsons*.

God's love launches our witness. We are designed to be evangelists who are first filled with the living water and who then offer that water to others. And we are offered the living water because of God's commitment to weak and fragile sinners. When we think that we have somehow "won" our relationship with God through our goodness, we miss the great need that our non-Christian friends have. Jesus came for the woman at the well. Because she was a sinner in need of much help, he embraced her and committed to her. That is why God chooses us as well. The fact that God pursues people like us brings much glory to Jesus' name.

PURSUED BY GOD

God taught me much about being chosen as I flew to Chicago to propose to Becky. As the airplane approached Chicago, I looked out my window and saw a cold, gray afternoon. I was overwhelmed by the massive buildings and wondered how many people were in Chicago that day. I wondered about the homeless people and how they could survive in such a cold city. The gray skies and the steel towers made Chicago feel ominous and lonely. And yet somewhere down there was my Becky. My soul was set on fire as I thought about finding her and committing my life to her that night.

As I looked from the airplane on our descent into Chicago, John 1:14 flashed into my mind. Jesus became flesh to dwell among us, and we beheld his glory. What was his trip to be with us like? Did he have thoughts similar to mine as he came to earth? Did he look upon the earth, full of pain and sorrow, violence and loneliness, and wonder where his bride was? As he walked up to the woman at the well that day, was he nervous? Could it be that Jesus practiced his speech as he walked the road to Sychar? I wonder if Jesus also carried the family diamond in his own pocket.

What Jesus do we know? What Jesus do we show? Do we experience Jesus as the woman at the well did, transparent and free from shame over our struggles and weaknesses? Do we know ourselves at the level of the woman at the well? It is safe to go there with Jesus. He is the great spiritual doctor who came for the needy and desperate. In him we are offered God's commitment to bring us to full healing. We are to be the healing that the world sees. His love is that powerful. His love is that good.

KEY CONCEPTS

Jesus the Bridegroom

- We are loved before we are sent for witness.
- Jesus is the fulfillment of God's promise to be the Bridegroom to Israel.
- The Bridegroom has arrived to claim his bride.

God's choosing the weak

- The Son did only what he saw the Father doing.
- Jesus was led by the Father to choose the woman at the well as his bride.
- He knew she was full of sin, pain and insecurity.
- God always chooses to lift the lowly and exalt the humble. That is great news for sinners like you, me and our friends.

Desperate for God, not religion

- When we are about relating with Jesus on the woman-at-the-well level, and when we learn to communicate our transformation, our non-Christian friends will see our relationship with Jesus and not just the exterior forms of religion.

GROWTH STEP

Take time to personally interact with the material from chapter one.

1. What words would you use to describe a healthy marriage?
2. Do those words describe your relationship with God?
3. What steps must you take to deepen your relationship with God?
4. Marriage is based on the spouses' loyalty and exclusive commitment to one another. Are you loyal to Jesus as your Bridegroom?
5. Are there other lovers you are giving your heart or life to?
6. What steps can you take to strengthen your loyalty to Jesus?

WHO WILL GIVE YOU PROPS?

We want gods that are not gods so we can "be as gods."

EUGENE PETERSON

We all want our proper respect (known as "props" in the hip-hop world today). We all want our reputations to go before us in positive ways. We all want that experience of cracking a smile when we overhear people making much of us. Liking to be liked is a central part of being a human being. So our question should never be, do we want someone to affirm us? We always will. Rather, the question should be, *who* are we looking to affirm us?

We cannot get props from everybody. Our world is full of people who are fundamentally at odds with one another. People have opposing views of God, politics, sexuality, money, technology and any other major area of life you can think of. One person in a certain community is regarded as a hero; that same person in another community is labeled diabolical. We can't please everyone, and if we try, we will lose ourselves in the process.

But oh, how we try! The desire to please just will not go away. If you don't think you are affected by this issue, ask yourself how you responded the last time you received criticism, even from a trusted friend. Did you thank God for someone who cared enough to point out your personal weaknesses to you so that you could grow? Or did you find your heart defensive and secretly come up with justifications for why the criticism was not accurate?

Today I received an e-mail from one of my best friends offering helpful critique on a sermon I recently preached. As I read the e-mail, my heart began to sink. I suddenly wondered if my friend, whom I esteem greatly, thought less of me because I was vague and not well prepared at the end of my sermon. I then found myself wanting to justify why the sermon wasn't as strong as it should have been. I wanted to tell him that I didn't have enough time to prepare for the assignment. Other justifications fell into line, raising their hands to be picked. Yet no matter how I looked at it, I couldn't get around it: I flat out did not want to hear critique today. Instead of helpful words that pointed out my weakness and growth areas, I wanted the shallow thrill of being told how wonderful I was. Can you relate?

The stakes are even higher for us as witnesses in an often hostile world. There will always be sections of the crowd that analyze us and try to tear us down. But we can stop spending time and emotional energy thinking about how to please them. The irony is that in relational evangelism, when we stop trying to please "the haters" in our world, they will often respect us much more because we have found something solid to build our lives upon. That's real.

Who will give us props? Someone will. The question is always who.

THE LOVE OF GOD DEEP WITHIN YOU

In the last chapter we looked at Jesus' immeasurable love and his rock-solid commitment to his people. It is his love, filling the hearts of his people, that enables someone like the woman at the well to stand before other people and testify that she has found the Savior. That is some serious love in action. The love of Christ in our hearts must be strong enough to overpower the love of the world. That is the battle you and I sign up for when responding to the call to be his witnesses. And that is the battle that will purify, deepen and strengthen our love for God. When we put ourselves in that place, the love of God will no longer be a nice side option; we will begin to *need* his love.

In John 5 the apostle begins to describe the persecution that came upon Jesus. In the first four chapters we read of little or no resistance as the Son of God's light exploded into the world. The light gave life to John the Baptist, fishermen, religious zealots, wedding parties, religious leaders and entire villages. But the tone and mood take a dramatic swing in John 5.

Jesus now stood before the religious leaders because he had healed the lame man at the pool. The religious leaders were focusing their interrogation on the claim that in healing the man Jesus broke the sabbath law. Jesus addressed the leaders—the very men who would eventually kill him—with these words about the hearts of men and women who long for love and affirmation:

> You search the scriptures because you think that in them you have eternal life; and it is they that testify on my behalf. Yet you refuse to come to me to have life. I do not accept glory from human beings. But I know that you do not have the love of God in you. I have come in my Father's name, and you do not accept me; if another comes in his own name, you will accept him. How can you believe when you accept glory from one another and do not seek the glory that comes from the one who alone is God? (John 5:39-44)

Jesus thus delivered an indictment against the religious leaders. But this teaching is also for his witnesses, because it describes our central temptation for why we would give up.

Jesus' argument is framed in the literary pattern called chiasm. You might think of this literary device as functioning like a sandwich. On the outside are the pieces of bread. As you get deeper into the sandwich, each piece inside the sandwich is mirrored by an equal or related piece on the opposite side. All of the pieces on the outside build up the argument for the main point in the middle. The main point supports and points outward to all of the other pieces. Here is the pattern for Jesus' teaching in John 5:

A. John the Baptist, the Father and the Scriptures testified to Jesus (5:31-39).

   B. The leaders refused to come to Jesus to have life (5:40).

      C. Jesus did not receive glory from people (5:41).

         D. The leaders did not have the love of God in them (5:42).

      C. The leaders could not believe, for they received glory from people (5:44).

   B. The leaders refused to seek the true glory that comes from God (5:44).

A. Witness came from Moses and the Scriptures (5:45-47).

The literary structure of John 5 captures a core set of issues involved with choosing to live in God's love. On the most outside piece of the chiasm (A) are the excellent witnesses who testified to Christ—John the Baptist, the Father, the Word and the prophet Moses. Jesus of Nazareth was not merely a rabbi; he was the fulfillment of God's mighty works for thousands and thousands of years. He was to be listened to. His testimony was true. The witnesses could not be stronger.

The next piece of evidence highlights the struggle of men and women (B). We all have a hard time coming to Jesus for life. We want to believe that life is found in seeking our own name, our own accomplishments or our own résumé that will give us glory. We will settle for the life that is not life if it will help us keep our facade up. When we come to Jesus, we admit that the resources for the spiritual life we long for are not found inside us. We don't want the glory that comes from God, because we want to be made much of. The praise of people costs less, is easier to secure and is always available. Therefore, we refuse to come to Jesus for life, thinking we already have life.

The third major piece of the chiasm stresses just how different Jesus is from you and me (C). Jesus does not receive glory from human beings. He knows that the glory of people is in direct opposition to the glory of God. He went so far as to warn that if we have the glory of people in our heart, we will not be able to believe in God.

Jesus knows that the glory of people is passing. The applause today might quickly turn into jeers tomorrow. Seeking glory from others is a terrible way to live our lives. We give the cheers and words of affirmation great power in our lives and are in turn controlled by them. We begin to perform for others, seeking their approval.

Jesus refuses to even get near that game. He has tasted the love of God. He knows which is better. He never receives glory from people. That is why he was able to turn a deaf ear to the crowds who chanted his name. That is why he was able to challenge Nicodemus in the night and not be tempted to join his elite religious club. That is why he was able to go to the cross. Glory from people does not appeal to Jesus in the least.

The heart of the teaching to the religious leaders was Jesus' declaration that they did not have the love of God inside them (D). In the control center of their soul there was a longing for God (what Blaise Pascal called a God-shaped vacuum), but they ignored it. They settled for the shallow claps of the crowd. And Jesus spotted that spiritual exchange a hundred yards away.

The clinching evidence that God's love was not in them was that they received praise from one another. If the love of God were in the soul, there would be no need for the praise of people. Why would a man with front-row tickets to the musical be outside, minutes before the show begins, buying tickets for the balcony? That is what the religious leaders did when they begged for praise from one another. This action only testified to what they did not have—the love of God. As John Piper says in his book *Future Grace*,

> Any love that we might achieve without God would not be true love because you cannot do lasting good for anyone without God. All the benefits of the world, minus God, would mean misery in the end. Moreover, achievements of compassion without God only feed the self-exalting ego; they are anathema to faith. Faith loves to experience all that God can do, not what self can do.

Instead of building on the solid foundation of God's love, the religious leaders built their lives on the fragile affirmations of others.

Jesus knows the human heart. He knows we are weak, frightened people who struggle every day. We wobble on the brink of emotional meltdown at one bad glare, one bad lane change on the freeway or one insensitive action from friend or foe. Jesus knows that our human hearts want us to be liked. This works well when befriending our world, but it does not work as well when the moment to challenge the world comes. The praise and applause we thought didn't mean much suddenly controls our behavior and acts as a filter to what we say. And unless our hearts are trained to love God more, they will be filled with the praise of mere mortals.

WHO WANTS TO PLEASE THE CROWDS?

Sitting down to watch my first episode of *Who Wants to Be a Millionaire?* I was immediately drawn into the gut-wrenching drama and the subplots of greed, intellectual pride and big cash. It was very entertaining.

The person on the hot seat was a lawyer from upstate New York. He had answered twelve questions correctly, using up his three lifelines to get there. He was currently at the $250,000 level and would reach $500,000 if he answered the next question correctly. If he missed the question, he would be herded off the stage with only a check for $32,000 to show for his efforts.

The $500,000 question was "Which single has spent the most consecutive weeks as the number-one song on the Billboard Top 100?" The options were songs by the Beatles, Whitney Houston, Boys II Men and Elvis Presley. The lawyer immediately confessed that he didn't know the answer, yet he continued exploring each thought that popped into his mind. He was beginning to crack under the pressure. Regis just looked on, wearing his trendy solid-on-solid outfit, and let the contestant squirm.

"Wow, Regis. This is really tough. I am not sure of the answer. I know that it's not Boys II Men or the Beatles. Ooh, this is a tough one. Man oh man."

Regis proved cooler than the other side of the pillow, saying little, all the while ushering in more pressure for the man to feel. The contestant shared vehemently his internal conflict for more than five minutes. Regis finally jumped in and asked the man for a decision. "What is your final answer?"

"Wow, $250,000 is a lot of money. That would pay for college for our two kids. We could also pay off the last of our mortgage. My wife and I want to travel. Wow, I don't know what to do. Regis, I think I am going to stop. I don't know the answer. That is too much money to leave on the table. I need to think about my future and my family."

Regis, with his piercing but innocent eyes, stared him down and asked him for the last time, "Is that your final answer?"

The man was just about to say yes when a faint voice from the audience peeled out, "C'mon, man, go."

Regis told the crowd to stay out of it and returned to the man. "Is that your final answer?"

The man, after being cheered on by the crowd, redirected his course and said, "No, Regis, I think I am going to go for it." The crowd let out a quick cheer, affirming his courage, preparing their own thirsty hearts for more drama and excitement. "Regis, the answer is C—Whitney Houston."

"Is that your final answer?"

"Yes. That is my final answer."

After what seemed like a week, Regis looked at the man and matter-of-factly said to him, "I am sorry. The answer is B. Boys II Men is the correct answer."

The crowd let out an agonizing sigh for the man. Regis then quickly wrapped up his experience. "Hey, thanks for playing. Here is a check for $32,000."

The man peeled himself from his chair, picked up his oversize cardboard check, and with the camera zooming in on his face, trudged the thirty-foot walk of shame off the stage. He looked like a prisoner entering his cellblock for the first time. He left humiliated. But at least he had pleased the crowd.

CHOICES AND CONSEQUENCES

From watching that episode, I learned how powerful the applause of the crowd can be. The lawyer from New York was obviously sensible and loved his family. He knew exactly what was at stake when he decided to go for $500,000. Yet one cheer from the crowd felled him. One clap in the dark from someone he would never meet caused him to betray his own reason and make one of the stupidest decisions of his life. Listening to the clap of that person in the dark cost him $218,000. I wonder if the man who cheered him on offered to help him pay his son and daughter's way to college.

If walking off the stage was tough for the lawyer, can you imagine how difficult it was for him to walk into his living room? What words could he possibly say to his family? "Sorry, honey, I didn't want that man to think I wasn't brave. Our mortgage isn't that important, is it?"

There are always consequences when we try to please the crowd. We choose moments of gratification, betraying the people and values we hold most dear. There is more power to the praise of people than we think.

As we ponder the choice to be people who seek to please God or please people, C. S. Lewis's famous words from *The Weight of Glory and Other Essays* have never been more appropriate:

> If there lurks in most modern minds the notion that to desire our own good and earnestly to hope for the enjoyment of it is a bad thing, I submit that this notion has crept in from Kant and the Stoics and is no part of the Christian faith. Indeed, if we consider the unblushing promises of reward promised in the

Gospels, it would seem that Our Lord finds our desires not too strong, but too weak. We are half-hearted creatures, fooling about with drink and sex and ambition when infinite joy is offered us, like an ignorant child who wants to go on making mud pies in a slum because he cannot imagine what is meant by the offer of a holiday at the sea. We are far too easily pleased.

Many of us choose the mud pies of human affirmation because we do not know what the holiday at the sea is like. Living the love of God is a real invitation to us. And the experience of rising above the games of the world and the power of people's words is every bit as exciting as taking a yacht to Jamaica for snorkeling—with the best chefs from the Food Channel on board supplying the eats! Jesus wants us to be his loyal, love-filled witnesses, not only for the sake of the gospel but also for the sake of our own joy and sanity.

LIVING THE LOVE OF GOD

Practically speaking, how do we fill our hearts with the love of God and reject the praises of people? How do we draw on the spiritual resources that are available to us to fight this seemingly unwinnable battle? I think our resources for this battle are threefold: (1) Jesus himself and his promises; (2) fellow witnesses in the community of faith; and (3) looking back at our own witness experiences to convince us that it is worthwhile to continue on as a witness.

First, we must begin with the end in mind. Living with Jesus in his kingdom is our end. Each day on this earth puts us one day closer to our destination. Do we envision meeting Jesus face to face? Do we have a picture in our mind of what we might to say to him—or more important, of what he will say to us? It is my deepest longing to hear from Jesus' mouth the same words that he spoke of John the Baptist in John 5: "He was a burning and shining lamp, and you were willing to rejoice for a while in his light" (John 5:35).

Jesus gives witness about his witnesses. He testified about what was good, right and of God in the life of John the Baptist. There is a great lesson in this verse. We were created for God's love and his affirmations to reign in our heart. Again, the question is, who will affirm us? Will we settle for the "mud pies" of people liking us? Or will we live by faith to reach the "holiday at the sea" of hearing Jesus' own testimony about loyal faith and confident witness? We were made to be filled with the love of God!

I think many of us might have a hard time imagining Jesus saying something positive about us and our Word-based evangelism ministries. Why is that? He spoke highly of many people in the Scriptures. He praised the centurion as having more faith than any person in Israel (Luke 7:9). He commended the woman with the flow of blood, calling her "daughter" and declaring that her faith had made her well (Mark 5:34). He even went so far as to publicly call his disciples his brothers (John 20:17). The Good Shepherd speaks words of praise, care and affirmation, not just words of challenge and critique. This is a central part of our heart being filled with his love. Without Jesus, his words of encouragement and the hope of being received by him, the words of men and women will have great power in our lives.

My soul longs to hear Jesus say, "Well done, good and faithful servant." It will be the very best to have Jesus affirm in me his own work, his light in my life transforming me into a lamp. I try every day to prepare for that day when I will meet Jesus. I want his testimony about John to be true of me. That is my end.

THE COMMUNITY OF FAITH

Jesus, in his wisdom, called people to follow him as a team. From the outset, he knew that we need encouragement from other people who have chosen to make the love of God their primary pursuit in life.

If we have the blessing of Christian community, it is a great gift from God. With others who love Christ, we have people who under-stand. We can share honestly with other Christians about our witness struggles and be encouraged and exhorted to faith. I have heard Christian community described as people who are skilled at putting spiritual Band-Aids on one another. Fellowship takes on entirely new dimensions when we need each other.

As we live as witnesses for Christ, we will be in a place of need. We will need to be refreshed. We will need to be renewed. We will need to be charged to choose courage. We will need to be told time and time again what is really true. We will need each other as we seek the love of God. We are on the frontlines, battling the enemy, and we need to hear from Jesus through each other. One word from Jesus can heal years of discouragement and pain. Often those words will come from the Christian community. If we are not hearing the voice of the Shepherd, we are vulnerable to the claps and cheers of the world.

LEGACY AND LOVE

As we test the waters of living as witnesses sent by God, we often focus on what we may lose if we are bold and faithful to our task. I would like us to focus on what we have to gain. A deep, lasting relationship is one of the chief blessings of being a witness.

People who are led to saving faith in Christ are forever grateful for those who shared with them the gospel of God's grace. Dave Palmer, the man who led me to faith ten years ago, is still one of my closest and truest friends, even though he now serves as a missionary on the other side of the world. He was the best man in my wedding and will always be among my dearest friends. Special friendships, like mine with Dave, are full of love, joy and life.

The apostle Paul knew such friendship. At the end of his letters, we are given glimpses into his vast network of kingdom relationships. Those relationships encouraged him and gave him life. For example, the last chapter of Romans is Paul greeting his friends. People were faithful to Paul because he was faithful to the gospel. They loved him, respected him and blessed him beyond measure because he was the person God had used to lead them to eternal life. He suffered greatly so that they might know Christ, yet out of that suffering grew wonderful Christian community.

I would rather have five people love me because of the gospel than have one hundred people like me because they think I am a nice guy. We must stop asking ourselves, *What will this person think of me if I share the gospel with him?* To be honest, the odds are that the person will think we are weird and will reject our message. So we shouldn't focus on being rejected by the hundred. Instead we should focus on the people God will bring to faith and on the relationships he will give us.

When we try to please our coworkers, our neighbors and our family, and therefore hold back our witness, we not only deny what is true but we also pass up the potential "holiday at the sea" of sharing the gospel with people like Timothy, Silas, Priscilla and Epaphroditus—people who might become our deepest friends and partners on the earth. These are the people who will become our own legacy and be among those who greet us when we enter into the eternal dwellings of God (Luke 16:9).

We are far too easily pleased.

FAITH AND MANAGING FEAR

So what do we do with the fear that is in our hearts every time we open our mouths to speak about Jesus? What do we do with our sweaty palms, clenched throats and the wild scenarios that run through our minds? First, we acknowledge that fear is a common experience in being a witness. God will then give us the encouragement we need to go on.

Paul was afraid and yet the New Testament suggests that he was a pretty good witness. God spoke to him in a vision, "Do not be afraid, but speak and do not be silent; for I am with you, and no one will lay a hand on you to harm you, for there are many in this city who are my people" (Acts 18:9-10). I take great confidence in the fact that Paul was scared—even on his second major missionary tour. God did not slam him for being scared but rather told Paul why he had nothing to fear. God will do the same for us.

The enemy of God, the devil, who abhors witness and the life that comes from it, tries to crush us by accusing us. He tells us that if we are afraid, we have already been defeated. Therefore we shut down our witness, thinking that victory is to proclaim the gospel fearlessly at the top of our lungs while standing on the desk in our office. That is not reality (and besides, our colleagues at work will likely scratch their heads). We will always have fear. The question we must ask is, will we manage our fear or will our fear manage us?

We do have a choice in this matter. We will never be fearless, but we can still be faithful while our fear is present. The first step is to know that what we feel on the inside is not broadcast to the world. Though our internal world may be screaming at a thousand decibels, our audience does not hear that. They will see and experience what we show them, and they only see our externals. If we are smooth on the outside, they will experience us as being smooth. If we allow our internal emotions to combust in our conversation, our audience will experience that as well. I do not consider this hypocrisy; Jesus himself encouraged his disciples, under certain circumstances, to have a face that masked their internal reality (Matthew 6:16-18).

Courage is grown as we look in the rearview mirror at our actions that cause us to move outside of our comfort zones. In the film *Three Kings*, Mark Wahlberg's character asks George Clooney's character how to manage his fear as they prepare to enter into a gun battle. Clooney looks Wahlberg in the eye and gives him some great advice: he will be scared and that is all right. The key is to do it. And then, when you look back, you will surprised at how brave you were.

The battle of faith is choosing the better portion—the choice that will put us one step closer to our final destination. Choosing faith and rejecting fear will be easier the more we do it. The first times we choose faith, amid the dry mouth, sweaty hands and racing heart, we will not feel like a hero. But later we will realize that God brought us through the test. We opened our mouth and stood our ground. We might have been rejected, but we are still in one piece. Fear will never go away, but as we manage it, it will become more manageable and we will become stronger witnesses to God.

IRIS LUCERO

My wife, Becky, moved to south-central Los Angeles in 1996 as a leader in a church plant committed to serving families in the inner city. During my first year in the neighborhood, she and I attended a dinner party where we met Iris Lucero, a twenty-two-year-old woman who attended junior college. Iris was socially gifted and made us feel at home with her Mexican cooking and hospitality. As dinner wound down, Becky and I chose to override our fears and investigate what God might be doing in Iris.

Actually, we kind of blurted out that we were Bible teachers at the college, then asked Iris and her family around the table if they read the Bible. It sure didn't come out as smoothly as we wanted. Nor was it the most creative, contextualized approach to evangelism. The moment of silence that followed our question seemed to go on for an hour.

Taking the lead, Iris shared that she had been trying to read God's Word but couldn't understand anything in it. She then rattled off five questions about God that had been on her mind. They were all excellent questions. We invited her to our neighborhood GIG, and she readily accepted. She was hungry for God.

At each of the first four GIG studies, the Word hit Iris deep in her heart. She said it was as if God had chosen each passage just for her, because each passage addressed a new issue she was dealing with during the week. It was a joy for us to see Jesus draw Iris in such a personal way.

After five GIG studies, Becky pulled Iris aside to invite her to become a disciple of Jesus. Iris was eager, understood what it meant and committed her life to Jesus. Not long after, Becky began a new disciples' study, where Iris could develop the habits and relationships that would help her to be more in love with Jesus in ten years. About the same time, Iris, a naturally and spiritually gifted evangelist, became a witness. Within a month, her entire extended family of two aunts, one uncle and their children became Christians. God was moving powerfully in and through Iris.

During that first season of Iris's faith life, our relationship with her was a great gift from God. She dubbed herself "BGI," which stood for "Baby Girl Iris." She called Becky her "Momma Becky," honoring Becky as the one who shared with her the words of life.

By living with the end in mind, Becky and I chose to be witnesses. We managed our fear and experienced the love of God that dwarfs the praise of people. We rejected the voices that said we would look stupid if we opened our mouth for the cause of Christ.

Each day is an opportunity to choose to have the love of God reign in our hearts. We must fight our fear to live the love of God. We never know who God is at work in. The only way to find out is to open our mouth. Don't settle for empty claps from the crowd. We were created for so much more.

KEY CONCEPTS

The love of God or the praise of people?

- The human heart receives life from the love of God or the praise of people, not both.
- God's love is more real than we think, as Jesus' words show.
- The praise of men and women is shallow and will always leave us unsatisfied.
- God's love is our end, and we must live our lives toward that end.

Legacy and love

- We often ask what we have to lose, not what we have to gain, if we witness.
- It is better to have five people love us for the gospel than to have one hundred love us because we are like them.
- Our witness might result in our most cherished friendships.

Managing fear

- Even the apostle Paul had fear as he shared his faith.
- Having fear is not the issue; the faith challenge is whether we will manage our fear.
- We often gather courage as we look in the rearview mirror.

GROWTH STEP

Think of one recent experience when you were afraid and chose not to engage someone with the gospel because of what that person might think of you.

1. How did fear manifest itself in your heart?
2. What was your greatest fear in talking to that person?
3. What Scripture might you use in the future to combat that fear?
4. Who could pray for you and apply a Band-Aid to your wound?
5. What lessons do you take from this experience?

THREE

WITNESS TO WORSHIP

I was willing to do anything . . . except evangelism.

MAITE RODRIGUEZ

The living God sends his people into the world for witness. The evangelistic message must be contextualized and delivered so that people will come to genuine faith in Jesus. Throughout the ages, the holy burden for the world's need of the gospel has sent missionaries to the ends of the earth to suffer greatly for the cause of Christ. The grace of God must be made known.

But how is Jesus' message of grace an experience of grace for his witnesses? We are well aware of how witness is good for the person or nation that is lost. I give personal testimony that my life has been rescued by the power of the gospel. But how is the delivery of witness good for the witnesses?

The apostle John knew witnessing holds great power to deepen worship in the disciple. John 5 includes the account of a lame man Jesus healed. This man did little to align himself further as a witness to Jesus' love and power. But then John 9 contains an account of another man, a blind man, whom Jesus healed. Unlike the lame man, the blind man embraced witness as a central experience in his life. The life consequences that came to each man crystallize the importance of witness in the life of a believer.

THE LAME MAN

John 5 begins with Jesus entering Jerusalem and immediately visiting a place where the outcasts and down-and-outers of the city lived.

> There was a festival of the Jews, and Jesus went up to Jerusalem.
> Now in Jerusalem by the Sheep Gate there is a pool, called in Hebrew Beth-zatha, which has five porticoes. In these lay many invalids—blind, lame, and paralyzed. One man was there who had been ill for thirty-eight years. When Jesus saw him lying there and knew that he had been there a long time, he said to him, "Do you want to be made well?" The sick man answered him, "Sir, I have no one to put me into the pool when the water is stirred up; and while I am making my way, someone else steps down ahead of me." Jesus said to him, "Stand up, take your mat and walk." At once the man was made well, and he took up his mat and began to walk. (John 5:1-9)

In *The IVP Bible Background Commentary: New Testament,* Craig Keener helps us understand that healing shrines were common throughout the ancient world. But Jesus, full of God's healing, mercy and power, took it upon himself to seek out a man who had been sick for a longer time than most at that time lived. The lame man had been paralyzed for thirty-eight years. He had sat at the pool day after day, watching others get well while his disability continued. Now he had his chance in a way he had never expected.

The man didn't know how to respond to the light that had suddenly broken into his life. He had no idea what Jesus had in store for him. And he wasn't sure how to respond. His facades were called into question as he interacted with someone far sharper and far more compassionate than the crowd he was used to.

As Jesus interacted with him, it became obvious that the man did not understand the power of God to transform his situation. But Jesus delivered a healing to him that caused his atrophied limbs to suddenly come to life and support him. The man was restored and walked out of the hospice to begin a new life.

This healing sparked a citywide controversy. The healed man was interrogated by the religious leaders, who asked what the man knew about Jesus. The leaders chose to focus on the fact that the healing took place on the sabbath. The man cooperated with all of their requests and went on to effectively turn Jesus over to the authorities for restoring his health. He had not the courage to stand up against the Jerusalem leaders nor the faith to cleave to God's sent One in his midst.

In contrast to the lame man, a blind man whom Jesus met stands out as one of the most courageous people in all Scripture. He is also the poster child for why witness is good for the witness. Instead of wilting under the pressure of conflict and interrogation, he excelled, developed and grew spiritually because of his afflictions.

THE BLIND MAN

A man who had been blind his whole life suddenly saw. You would think receiving his physical sight after living his entire life in darkness would be amazing enough. But Jesus had even more grace for the man—he offered him spiritual sight. And that grace came through witness.

As [Jesus] walked along, he saw a man blind from birth. His disciples asked him, "Rabbi, who sinned, this man or his parents, that he was born blind?" Jesus answered, "Neither this man nor his parents sinned; he was born blind so that God's works might be revealed in him. We must work the works of him who sent me while it is day; night is coming when no one can work. As long as I am in the world, I am the light of the world." When he had said this, he spat on the ground and made mud with the saliva and spread the mud on the man's eyes, saying to him, "Go, wash in the Pool of Siloam" (which means Sent). Then he went and washed and came back able to see. The neighbors and those who had seen him before as a beggar began to ask, "Is this not the man who used to sit and beg?" . . .

They brought to the Pharisees the man who had formerly been blind. . . .

The Jews did not believe that he had been blind and had received his sight until they called the parents of the man who had received his sight and asked them, "Is this your son, who you say was born blind? How then does he now see?" . . .

For the second time they called the man who had been blind, and they said to him, "Give glory to God! We know that this man is a sinner." . . .

Jesus heard that they had driven him out, and when he found him, he said, "Do you believe in the Son of Man?" He answered, "And who is he, sir? Tell me, so that I may believe in him." Jesus said to him, "You have seen him, and the one speaking with you is he." He said, "Lord, I believe." And he worshiped him. (John 9:1-8, 13, 18-19, 24, 35-38)

The religious leaders here, as in the case of the lame man, investigated the miracle. They focused their interrogation on Jesus kneading the clay—a violation of the Pharisaic sabbath law. In the heat of his conversations with the religious leaders, the blind man held his ground. With no theological training or evangelism seminars, he became a witness and began walking his road to true spiritual sight. He gained boldness, theological insight, communication confidence, and even sarcastic dramatic ability *as* he witnessed.

The blind man's healing was twofold. He saw his physical world, but then he began to perceive the spiritual world. Witness was the trigger and accelerator to his spiritual sight. As if being fitted with new lenses during each round of interrogation, he began to see Jesus more and more clearly. Jesus was first unknown to him. He knew his

name but did not know where he was. After the next round of witness, he recognized Jesus as a prophet. Witness brought even greater
focus, as he proclaimed to the Pharisees that Jesus was sent from God
and began to define himself as Jesus' disciple. He followed Jesus even
though it meant being banned from participating in the local religious life.

John tells us that, once the man was cast out of society, Jesus
"found him," which means he looked for him. He likely peered
down the streets of Jerusalem, asking people if they had seen him.
Jesus fulfilled the promise of the shepherd from Psalm 23 by actively chasing the man down with goodness and lovingkindness.
Upon finding him, Jesus rewarded his witness by revealing his
own divinity.

Once he saw the glory of God, worship was the formerly blind
man's only response. Jesus did not rebuke him for worshiping him
as if he were breaking one of the Ten Commandments. He received the man's worship. The blind man thus became the first
person to worship Jesus in the Fourth Gospel. He worshiped him
long before the twelve apostles did. After being sought out by Jesus
and worshiping him, I imagine the sting of persecution quickly left
him. But the spiritual healing that came through witness blessed
him forever.

A TALE OF TWO HEALINGS

John wanted us to compare and contrast the lame man and the
blind man. (I am indebted to Alan Culpepper's book *Anatomy of
the Fourth Gospel* for helping me see John's intentions in the par-
allel accounts of the lame man and the blind man.) John wrote
with the intention of our putting them side by side so that we can
learn how disciples grow in their understanding of and passion for
Jesus. When we study their stories in tandem, we realize their experiences with Jesus were nearly identical.

Lame Man	Blind Man
Jewish festival (5:1)	Jewish festival (5—11 context)
Physical illness (5:5)	Physical illness (9:1)
Length of illness (5:5)	Length of illness (9:1-3)
Water—Pool of Bethesda (5:2)	Water—Pool of Siloam (9:7)
Healing initiated by Jesus (5:6)	Healing initiated by Jesus (9:6)
Jesus' knowledge of ailment (5:6)	Jesus' knowledge of ailment (9:3)
Jesus' failure to touch him (5:8)	Jesus' failure to touch him (9:7)
Instant healing (5:9)	Instant healing (9:7)
Interrogation by Jewish leaders (5:10)	Interrogation by Jewish leaders (9:15)
Second search by Jesus (5:14)	Second search by Jesus (9:35)

Every incident in the healing of one man parallels an incident in the experience of the other man. This is not an accident. The apostle John wanted us to understand that there was no difference between the experiences these men had with Jesus. What *was* different was what was in their heart and how they responded to the call of becoming a witness.

Lame Man	Blind Man
Love of the praise of people (5:15)	Love of the affirmation of God (9:33)
Honor by the Jewish leaders (5:15)	Removal from the synagogue (9:34)
Persecution of Jesus (5:16)	Worship of Jesus (9:38)

How is each man in these stories remembered?

The lame man will always be remembered as the man who was given a miraculous healing but who lost the lasting benefit because he was a coward. He started the persecution that led to Jesus' execution, and he believed the system he was in offered him a better future than did Jesus. He destroyed his future because he chose not to witness. The lame man is our negative example, a model of faithlessness to be pitied but avoided at all costs.

The blind man, on the other hand, will forever be honored as the courageous witness who rose above adversity. He endured high levels of persecution and stood firm in what is true, scorning his present sys-

tem for the security of Jesus. Unlike the lame man, the blind man se-
cured his future because of his witness. He serves as our model of
courage and spiritual growth.

Witness is not a side issue in the life of Jesus' disciples. It is *the* issue!
It is the only difference between one person rejecting Jesus and another worshiping him. Therefore, the call to become a witness is full
of God's grace. Of course, this is true for all of God's commands. I like
how Darrell Johnson put it in a sermon he delivered at Glendale Presbyterian Church: "God speaks the commandments to protect and en-
hance the life of freedom given to us by grace." Certainly the call to
become a witness presupposes the grace of God in our lives. But God's
grace does not stop with merely a healing. The man at the pool, thinking everything was fine, closed his heart in betrayal and was visited by
Jesus with an exhortation to stop sinning. Witness is given for the good
of the world, but it is also a command, dripping with grace, for the disciples, so that we might experience more of Jesus.

Witness, and potential suffering from that witness, cannot be removed from the spiritual life of the disciple. Witness is a tried and
true model of how God turns emotionally fragile reeds into durable,
trustworthy rocks. The man who was born blind became a person of
great character after four rounds of interrogation and witness. John
Piper, in his book *Let the Nations Be Glad*, describes the goodness of
suffering-filled witness this way:

> The death of Christ for the sin of my selfishness is not meant to
> help me escape the suffering of love but to enable it. Because
> he took my guilt and my punishment and reconciled me to
> God as my Father, I do not need to cling any longer to the com-
> forts of the earth in order to be content. I am free to let things
> go for the sake of making the supremacy of God's worth known.

When we remove witness, we are left with disciples who have not
been tested in the fires of affliction. We are left with people who have

been touched by Jesus but have not loyally aligned themselves with Jesus. The opening of our mouths for witness prevents us from becoming fence riders who live at the whims of worldly cares and passions. Witness is where disciples are turned into citizens of the kingdom of God.

Where there is great witness, of course, there is great worship. The witnesses who pay costs hold more closely to Jesus because they have given everything else away. These are the saints who experience the true delight of his bread and the spiritual satisfaction of his water. They know Jesus more deeply because of their witness that leads to suffering. I fear that much of our worship today is rooted in Jesus' providing life blessings and not in costly witness. The worshiper who thanks God for a new laptop does not come near the level of worship of the person who has just lost her job because she was a witness.

SPECIALIZED DISCIPLESHIP

Witness is never to be a side option of discipleship or an elective for the people who are "gifted" for it. Do we view evangelism as central and vital to our own spiritual growth? Until we understand the power of witness to create worshipers, and to re-create that passion over and over again, we will be tempted to keep evangelism on the edges of our programs and leadership training.

Major league baseball mirrors Christian ministry in how it has become specialized. Back in the old days, pitchers were tough, durable. Unless his team was getting beaten like a rented mule, the starting pitcher would stay on the mound until the seventh inning. There were not many relief pitchers, because it was expected that the pitcher would pitch until his arm fell off. But in today's game, pitchers have become specialists. The use of relief pitchers has become one of the most strategic elements of the game, and baseball teams spend millions of dollars for pitchers who will be used only in specific situations.

For example, many left-handed relief pitchers are brought into the game only to face the opponent's best left-handed hitter. My favorite team, the Los Angeles Dodgers, currently employs a forty-six-year-old left-handed pitcher who usually faces only one or two batters in a game. Just last week I saw him pitch in an ESPN classic game from 1986. Though he's almost fifty, he's still going strong. But because of today's sophistication, this is his only role. The development and training of relief pitchers reflects their specialized call.

Many relief pitchers have confessed that their approach to the game is far from rigorous. They relax every night in the bullpen because they know they will not be called on until the late innings. And even then, they will face only one or two batters. On ESPN recently, one relief pitcher for the Cleveland Indians confessed that his regular game-day routine includes watching television, joking with his teammates, eating sunflower seeds and sneaking an ice cream bar every night during the sixth inning.

I fear that the specialization of Christian ministry roles causes a lack of zeal in our pursuit of Jesus. Our sophistication shields us from the great challenges of witness. People feel like they could not possibly be called to be a witness, because they are in charge of music, small groups, snacks, supervising evangelism and other worthy servant roles. But as we narrow our scope, it becomes harder to see how witness is for our good. Witness becomes a trendy appetizer, not the entrée for our ministries. Therefore, the challenge set before many disciples is small and the preparation and training do not challenge anyone. We find ourselves with ministries full of "players" who have no problem eating ice cream bars during the "game" because they know there is a one-in-one chance they will not be called in to take a central role. As we embrace the compartmentalized life of the disciple, we create discipleship environments of comfort and ease. Our focus and call have become so limited that we are "eating ourselves" into spiritual apathy.

Witness as discipleship must be a part of our lives—for the sake of our own souls. In our churches, campus ministries and mission organizations, it is as if entire subsections of people are "protected" from Jesus' call to be a witness. Unless someone is a young apostle Paul, gifted in the way of the street preacher, it seems widely accepted that Jesus is not calling him or her into active evangelism. There is a great downside of losing witness as a central expression of discipleship. Without witness, our mission becomes reduced to caring for Christians. Jesus has more than that for all of us. The call to witness is not to be an afterthought in the life of a disciple of Jesus. It is not for a select few. Witness is a gift of grace from God for the disciple and for the spiritually blind world.

THE EFFECTS OF GOOD AND BAD LEADERSHIP

When I think of witness as discipleship, two people come to my mind: Rachel Sims and Maite Rodriguez. Both were under my leadership in campus ministry at different times. Both are gifted, outgoing women. But because I've learned some things about leadership over the years, my influence on their witness turned out to have very different results.

Rachel has the kind of personality that is bigger than the room. As a freshman in college, she had just come back from an international summer mission and was zealous to share her faith with the entire campus. Under my leadership, though, her passion for evangelism waned. I chose to focus more on what I perceived as Rachel's weaknesses, because I thought that in doing so I was discipling her. So I encouraged Rachel to be more contemplative and more thoughtful and to grapple with the true issues of following Jesus. She became a small-group leader and spent two of her four years at college taking care of Christians. She then graduated, joined the local church and became a small-group leader at the church. Within a few short years, evangelism—which at one point had been her great passion—was nowhere to be found in Rachel's life. I did little to encourage, support or train her to be an effective witness. I could have learned from Jesus about discipling others.

As I studied the account of the blind man, I found myself asking where Jesus went. Through the first eight chapters of John, Jesus is the dominant character in every scene. Yet in chapter 9 he noticeably retreats into the shadows. What we see in his absence is one of his philosophies of discipleship development. Jesus grew his witnesses by working in their lives and then sending them into the world to bear witness to the truth. The spiritual development of the blind man came because Jesus watched him give witness to hostile friends, family and religious leaders. Jesus did not protect him. Where would the blind man have been in his own development if Jesus had jumped in merely because the man was suffering? Jesus loved the man so deeply that he sat back and watched him endure the persecution that would eventually lead to the perfection of his spiritual sight.

When was the last time we instructed those we mentor to grow closer to Jesus by proclaiming witness in hostile crowds? When was the last time we saw one of our emerging leaders being bruised and battered emotionally or physically for the sake of witness and let that leader go a couple more rounds? I think our temptation is to keep our leaders in the safety of Christian small groups and meetings. Why don't we send them out for witness for their growth? Jesus did not jump in to stop the process of persecution in the name of protecting his disciple. Jesus did not develop his disciples with kid gloves on. He let them grow into who they were to become *through* the process of witness.

Rudy Giuliani, when mayor of New York City, kept a placard on his desk that read, "I'm responsible." He also had two paintings in his office, both by the Italian painter Ambrogio Lorenzetti. The first painting was titled *The Effects of Bad Government on City Life*, while the second painting was titled *The Effects of Good Government on City Life*. Giuliani used the placard and the paintings to motivate himself and remind himself that he was responsible for the development of his people. In the same way, we are responsible for the development of our people.

If I were to follow the former mayor's model, I would have my own pictures. The first would be titled *The Effects of Bad Leadership on Jesus' Disciples*. I would hang a picture of Rachel to remind me that disciples are made strong through witness. The second picture would be titled *The Effects of Good Leadership on Jesus' Disciples*. I would hang a picture of Maite under that title, reminding me that disciples are made strong through witness.

MAITE RODRIGUEZ

Maite Rodriguez is a nineteen-year-old student from the Claremont Colleges in Los Angeles who came to know Jesus more deeply and more intimately because of learning to be a witness. Here's her story.

> Sarah was also a freshman and she lived next door to me. She and her roommate had major relational problems, and by the end of the first semester, one of them had to move out. I thought about opening up my room to Sarah but then quickly dismissed the idea when I thought about the costs of living with her. That night in my dorm Bible study we studied Luke 10, the parable of the good Samaritan. It became clear to me that God was telling me that I needed to care for Sarah as the Samaritan cared for the man on the road. The next night God confirmed his message to me by having our fellowship meeting be on the good Samaritan as well. I was sold. I couldn't believe that God was showing up and giving me real direction for what to do. This was totally new to me, so after the talk I

went up to the speaker and thanked him, because the message was my final confirmation that God wanted me to take
this action. After I told him more about the situation, he said
to me, "I would encourage you, when you tell those girls
about your decision to swap, to use it as an opportunity to
share with them about Jesus."

Say what? I had never done anything like that before. I had
never "shared about Jesus." As a matter of fact, I had told the
woman who was discipling me that evangelism was the one
thing I was not interested in doing. I had a hard enough time
just saying that I was a Christian. I was terrified of stepping on
toes and burning bridges like I had seen happen so many times
as a youth. But I realized that if I wasn't straight up about why
I was choosing to move, then they would think that I had chosen to act kindly on my own, which would be a lie, because it
took multiple undeniable signs from God to spur me to this decision. So that very night I went back to my dorm, gave myself
a pep talk the whole way back and headed up to our hall to give
Sarah the news.

The two of us were alone in the hallway when I suggested we
room together, and she threw her arms around me out of excitement and relief. Just when I thought I was in the clear and
wouldn't have to tell her about how I had changed my mind,
she asked me, "Maite, why are you doing this? What changed?"
With my voice shaking, I blubbered, "Umm, well, it's just that
. . . See, I kind of feel like . . . The way I see it . . . Honestly,
Sarah, I think that God told me to move in with you, so I'm going to." She looked at me half puzzled and half surprised, then
shrugged and said, "Well, whatever. I'm just glad you're moving in." That shaky explanation was my first step of faith in the
area of evangelism.

As we became better friends and roommates, my steps of

faith became more frequent and more bold. I started putting two and two together in my mind. Sarah had these struggles, and Jesus had these answers, and since I knew them both, I should let her in on the goods. It wasn't an overnight change, but I started by just bringing up Jesus more in our conversations. I began to tell her if I was going to Bible study or fellowship, whereas before I would just sneak off without telling anyone so I wouldn't have to feel awkward. And one day, when Sarah was in tears over the overwhelming pressure that comes with being pre-med, I offered to pray for her, and she let me!

In the spring of that year, I began attending IVCF evangelism training for students in Los Angeles. During that time, I began to realize that the situation with Sarah was no accident, but in fact, God was weaving together quite an amazing story. It wasn't a freak occurrence that I moved in with Sarah. I was sent to her. And God's purpose in this was not just to make me more of a risk taker but to draw her to himself and into his kingdom. It was time for me to step up and take seriously what he had been working out since the beginning.

So one night we were both in bed, and our late-night conversation led to the topic of God. She had been reading this New Age book about how everything in your life is connected and there are signs everywhere. It was pitch-black dark in the room, and everything seemed calm, but I felt like my heart was going to pop out of my body, it was pounding so hard. I had this unnerving feeling that God was not going to let me fall asleep until I took this next step and asked her if she wanted to do a GIG with me. So I took a deep breath and asked if she'd be interested in taking a look at what Jesus had to say about some of those things. She answered easily, "Sure, when can we start?"

Our GIGs were rich in discussion about Jesus and in sharing stories of how our lives connected. Sarah just loved learning about Jesus. She soaked in the stories of his life and always wanted to go deeper. So when IV's One Day with God conference for non-Christians at Catalina rolled around, she was eager to experience Jesus on a deeper level. The first night that we were on the island, Sarah prayed for a sign. She told me she couldn't trust that Jesus was someone she could give her life to unless she had some proof. She told me bluntly, "I am a science major, so I just need some evidence."

The following morning the conference speaker taught out of John 6, where Jesus proclaims, "I am the bread of life. He who comes to me will never go hungry, and he who believes in me will never be thirsty." The whole talk was about bread—bread stories, bread symbolism, bread, bread, bread. Halfway through, it hit me. My mind flashed back to our boat ride over to Catalina. Sarah and I had played a word game on the boat. Of all the words in the dictionary, the one that she had picked was *bread*. And because I messed up the game, we randomly got into this long conversation about bread. So as I'm sitting listening to the Word, this connection dawns on me and I look over at Sarah. Tears are streaming down her cheeks and she looks at me, smiles, and mouths, "Bread." Sarah was amazed that God had given her the sign before she even asked for it.

At the evening session, when the evangelist called for those who wanted to come alive like Lazarus to stand, Sarah went up strong. Unashamed and boldly, she stood up to commit her life to Jesus. I could not contain myself as I sat next to her, trembling from joy. I had never seen such a beautiful thing, and I knew that I'd never be the same. This was even better than when I became a Christian!

After the public time of commitment, Sarah and I went to pray together, and in the most sincere way possible Sarah said to her new Lord, "Jesus, I want you to be my bread of life." When I heard those words, I felt like the maid of honor at my best friend's wedding, savoring each word of her loving vow.

Sarah's conversion is the deepest experience of Jesus I've had in my entire life. I have never had more of a reason and desire to worship than I did then when Sarah committed to Jesus. Through Sarah I have learned that Jesus is capable of anything. I want to live my life as a witness for Jesus. In that will come my deepest joy.

That testimony was from Maite's freshman year. This next testimony came from the fall of her sophomore year. Notice the depth that developed in her over the course of the year because of her commitment to being a witness.

I have really grown as someone who is able to challenge my friends to consider Jesus. I have realized that, deep in me, I love following Jesus . . . up until the point where I could possibly be criticized for it. But when you challenge people, this definitely involves making yourself vulnerable to criticism and at times even flat-out rejection. But I've learned that it is a major point of growth for people, and much growth in God seems to come from points of challenge.

Maite embodies the truth that life lived as a witness leads us afresh to the feet of Jesus. May we never settle for the cowardly path of the lame man. May we instead follow the courageous model of the blind man into the discipleship growth that comes only through costly witness. Through tension and turmoil, we see Jesus more and more clearly, and our worship will become hotter and deeper. Witness and worship await us.

KEY CONCEPTS

The lame man or the blind man?

- Both men, with nearly identical circumstances, experienced Jesus' power for healing.
- The only difference between these two men was how they handled witness.
- Witness is as much for the witness as for the lost world.

Specialized disciples

- Witness is often seen as a side order and not an entrée for spiritual growth.
- Discipleship has become specialized and witness is not expected or called for.

Our responsibility

- Jesus developed his people by leading them into tough situations.
- Rachel is an example of the effects of bad leadership on Jesus' disciples.
- Maite is an example of the effects of good leadership on Jesus' disciples.

GROWTH STEP

Think of one evangelistic relationship that you have been involved with during your lifetime.

1. How did Jesus disciple you through your witness relationship?
2. What suffering did you experience because of your witness?
3. What was the outcome of your witness for your friend?
4. How did you come to see Jesus more clearly because of your witness?
5. What was your experience of Jesus because of your witness?

SEEKERS
OR SNACKERS?

*You preach what you need to hear. You sing your life,
and you want it to count, I suppose. I'm hoping people are tired
of singers whose mouths are filled with words that were written for
them and they don't believe. Their arms and legs move in
directions that other people choreograph.*

BONO

He will not be a wise man who does not study the heart of man.

CHARLES SPURGEON

Jesus was truly the master of this world. His days were full of challenge at every turn, yet he never once was sent reeling backward. No Gospel mentions his getting caught off-guard. When those who hated him launched their complex tests and trials, Jesus quickly turned the tables with the perfect response. When the demonized, diseased and disenfranchised threw themselves at him, he not only met the need of the moment but also restored the dignity that had been taken from them. No matter who it was or what the situation, Jesus knew how to handle the world. Jesus was a great leader.

What questions did Jesus ask when he met new people? I wonder if, as people came to him, Jesus asked himself whether they trusted in themselves or knew they needed help. Did they come recognizing their cavernous spiritual needs, or did they come thinking that for the most part things were going along all right? Were they confident because of their status in the society, or were they willing to cash in everything for a second chance?

The first followers were fishermen, tax collectors and outcasts. We don't hear a great deal about the needs of the fishermen at the beginning of the Gospel of John, but by the end, we become all too familiar with the needs of their souls. Yet Jesus called them to himself. The tax collector was someone who probably didn't like himself much, on account of what he did. Yet Jesus offered him a new life. The woman at the well, the man who was lame for thirty-eight years, the woman caught in adultery and the man born blind were all outcasts in one form or another. Yet Jesus showed tender love and compassion toward all of them. And in starting relationships with them, he taught them to believe that God was for them and that they could start over in life.

The people Jesus challenged more directly were the ones who hid their needs behind religious masks. In John 2 we read that a crowd believed in Jesus after the temple cleansing because of his signs. Jesus responded by not giving his heart to them, because he knew what was in theirs. In John 3 we see how Nicodemus came at night with the good news that he and the other religious leaders had finally figured Jesus out and had decided to allow him to join their elite club. Though Jesus was likely younger than Nicodemus, Jesus blasted his elder for spiritual arrogance and ignorance (a reaction that proved critical to Nicodemus's own conversion later in the book). In knowing self-sufficient religious people, Jesus motivated them to believe that they didn't know God as well as they thought they did and that they needed to start over in life.

The people who came with their needs fully exposed in the light received compassion and mercy. The people who came with their needs concealed in the dark were challenged by Jesus' words to stop playing religious games. He always said the right thing. Jesus is the great evangelist!

MY OWN CONFUSION

In my own dealings with the world, I often get confused about who is the enemy. For a variety of reasons, I often forget to ask the important questions about where people are coming from. That is not Jesus' way.

When Jesus walked the earth, he knew people deep down in the soul, where it counts. He knew what they needed. And whether they were zealous in their religion or flagrantly immoral, Jesus demonstrated the courage to love them with the word that was perfect for them. No matter from what direction they arrived, Jesus always pointed them to their next step to know God. Jesus, full of grace and truth, gave everyone who came into contact with him a large dose of both.

I wish I would have thought about how Jesus handled people when I went to a recent Bob Dylan concert. I wish I would have asked if the person I was interacting with needed a word of challenge or a word of compassion. Unfortunately I chose the wrong way of handling the world. And I ended up feeling torn up about the whole situation.

A friend and I, major Bob Dylan fans, bought tickets to his show and eagerly waited for the concert night. When the big night finally came, we were down in the pit, standing with Dylan's most faithful fans. Many had traveled internationally just for the show and knew every word to the twenty songs on the playlist. They sang the songs in an almost reverent manner. Except for one woman. She was in her mid-forties and very drunk. She was flailing about, dancing wildly, even to slow songs. She bumped into me once, slurred out incoherencies and even got angry at me for being in her way. She bumped me again.

Was she someone who needed a challenge or a kind word? Instead of asking why this middle-aged woman was drunk and trying to get everyone's attention, I condemned her in my heart. I did not respond with compassion. I could only think how unfortunate it was that I had to stand next to her at the concert of a lifetime.

If I had known the world like Jesus knows the world, I would have had compassion on this woman's pain that led to drunkenness and insecure behavior. I know it was a concert, so engaging in a deep conversation was not an option, but maybe God put her in front of me so that I would pray for her, breaking the kingdom of light into her darkness. But that night I was unable to get over my own impatience and critical spirit, so I condemned her in my heart and did nothing to be a part of her spiritual healing.

One of the greatest challenges in dealing with worldlings is that they are a complex people. They are often proud and competent but also fragile and tender. They are at once thoughtful and spiritually unaware. If we are to have compassion on the world, then focusing on people's spiritual needs and their lack of knowledge of the truth is a good place to start. That is where the apostle John started in teaching us how Jesus handled the world. If they fundamentally don't know anything about God, how can we be critical and harsh with them?

THE WORLD IS SPIRITUALLY UNINFORMED

The great prologue to the Gospel of John tells us that the world was created by the Son of God and yet the world did not know him (John 1:1-18). The world is uninformed—that is where John wanted us to start so that we will not be afraid of the world. Time and again, the apostle directed us to the crowds' lack of knowledge when it came to Jesus. He used the tongue-in-cheek device of irony to shame the world. He gave the readers little winks, reminding us of who we are dealing with, so that we will not be overwhelmed by externals and fall into a callous or fear-filled life.

Consider the following snapshots from Alan Culpepper's book *Anatomy of the Fourth Gospel* of how John framed the testimony of the crowd. Each testimony is ironic because the person's testimony was actually true on a surface level but incredibly false on the spiritual level.

1:46   Can anything good come out of Nazareth?

2:10   Everyone serves the good wine first. . . . But you have kept the good wine until now.

4:12   Are you greater than our ancestor Jacob?

6:52   How can this man give us his flesh to eat?

8:22   Is he going to kill himself? Is that what he means by saying, "Where I am going, you cannot come"?

8:53   Are you greater than our father Abraham, who died?

9:40   Surely we are not blind, are we?

18:38 What is truth?

John 2:1-11 gives us a great example of the ignorance of the world. Jesus was invited to a wedding at Cana where the wine ran out. At the request of his mother, Jesus miraculously transformed more than one hundred gallons of stale water into the kind of wine people on the Food Channel drool over. Yet as the living God moved powerfully in the world, who knew it? The majority of the guests left the wedding unaware that a miracle had been performed and a sign had been given. The only testimony they heard was the steward of the feast proclaiming the generosity of the groom for serving the good wine last.

The steward of the feast is the focal point of John's literary wink. The apostle wanted us to scratch our head and yell at the man, "No, you have it all wrong!" The steward's testimony was true in that it was indeed a unique individual who had served the good wine last. But he spotlighted and gave honor to the wrong person.

He should not have been bearing witness about the groom; he should have been testifying about Jesus of Nazareth. *He* was the source of the wine. Meanwhile, the Lord, operating within the framework of his larger plan, allowed the man to give false testimony. Maybe Jesus even applauded the groom for his splendid act of hospitality!

If we see the world as clearly as Jesus does, we will treat people differently. Consciously or subconsciously, we often frame our non-Christian friends as hardened people who understand the gospel and yet reject it. But the reason most of our friends do not follow Jesus is because they have never heard the true gospel. Most have no idea what Jesus offers them. Paul's words in Romans 10 are entirely true of our current situation. How will non-Christians believe unless they hear the Word of God? And how will they hear unless speakers of God's Word are sent to them?

Seeing the world as spiritually unaware should affect our relationships within the world. I believe this foundation point for relational evangelism should cause two reactions in God's people: we are to be filled with compassion at the pain and emptiness that are the fruit of living life apart from the living God, and we are to be empowered to teach the words of Jesus that are eternal life.

BIBLICAL ILLITERACY AND WITNESS

The world does not know Jesus' message. A majority of our friends did not grow up going to church. Instead of learning Gospel stories as children, they watched cartoons on television. They are not able to name the twelve apostles, but they are able to tell us when Eminem's new video debuts on *Total Request Live*.

We have such a hard time engaging non-Christians because we are in entirely separate cultures. Today's witnesses must be as comfortable and knowledgeable with the music on MTV, the guests on the *Today* show and whatever else the world is discipled in. We must be relevant. It is on us, the Christians, to bridge the gaps in culture and communication. This is one application of Jesus' prayer that his disciples would not be removed from the world but rather would be protected from the evil one (John 17:15).

Worldly people think they know what Christians are all about. And Christians think they know what the world is all about. We need to meet in the middle, and God's Word is our great point of connection. Until unbelievers get a clear understanding of the Word and what God is really about, they will make their decision to stay away from Christ based on the most unlikely pieces of evidence.

Do you know why your friends do not go to church? Do you know why they seem uninterested in the things of God? I bet the answers would surprise you.

I first met Jim my senior year in high school. He was in his mid-twenties and was slowly working his way through junior college. We worked together, were teammates on a softball team and partied hard together. Jim went to church with his parents a couple of times a year, but you wouldn't have guessed it, for he would wake up every other morning wondering how he had driven home from the bar the night before.

After my transformation by Jesus, I returned from college passionate to teach my friends about the Lord. I invited Jim to my GIG that summer. He came faithfully all summer, even hosting the GIG at his parent's house once or twice. At the end of our fourth study, he pulled me aside to ask me a question: "John, I have really enjoyed the GIGs, but why don't we do one that is really important?"

I replied, "Jim, I would love to do one that is really important. Which one would you want to do?"

"How about John 3:16? I have always wondered what that meant."

I asked him, "What do you think John 3:16 means?"

Jim replied, "I think it means, 'Stop watching football and go to church!' And the thing that really gets me is how hypocritical

all those church people are—they are at the football games holding signs when they should be at church. That's why I don't go to
church."

A window suddenly opened to me when I realized that Jim's
only exposure to John 3:16 was seeing someone holding up a sign
at professional football games. Somehow Jim had pieced it together that the Bible was written with pro football in mind and
that it even had a verse that condemned watching football on
Sundays. In his mind he saw the sign holders as the most egre-
gious of all hypocrites because they were disobeying their own
message. They were such bold hypocrites that they held the sign
at the football games!

I didn't know how to respond to Jim. I wanted to sarcastically say
that God could not possibly be against football, because so many
players pray to him after knocking a man out cold or scoring a touch-
down. But I didn't. Instead I told him that he had gotten the meaning
of John 3:16 wrong and that though I myself had only just recently
learned what it meant, I would be more than happy to teach him
what I knew.

That day God changed how I view my non-Christian friends.
Granted, we will come across those who are well educated with
God's Word and still reject Jesus' message. But those individuals
are harder to come by these days. Our future will be filled with
people who don't know the treasures of spiritual wealth found in
the Bible. John 3:16 might as well be in the original Greek language for them. To make matters worse, they are bombarded by
cultural assumptions and half-truths that further steepen their slip-
pery slope into thinking the gospel is irrelevant. After my conversation with Jim, I dedicated myself to loving my friends by helping
them see what the Bible really teaches. I wanted them to have
enough accurate information so that they might have a chance to
follow God.

THE SEEDBED OF BOLDNESS

Instead of seeing the world as a modern-day Goliath — standing ten feet tall, wielding weapons we could never lift, laughing at us — may we view our world as a piece of clay that is waiting to be shaped. The world is not as bad as we think it is. It is unaware and is more open to God than we think. Will we walk into the spiritual leadership vacuum that every non-Christian experiences? Or will we allow MTV and ESPN to disciple the nations? When we begin to live boldly and insightfully for evangelism, many doors will be open for effective witness.

We are not to be threatened and made cowards by the world. Viewing the world as perishing for lack of knowledge of God is the seedbed of boldness. We have nothing to be afraid of. We must keep the world's need to be taught the gospel at the forefront of our witness. We cannot forget that the world is ignorant and that we have the gospel that will save people's souls. God sends us into the world to be his heralds of the life and death to come.

When we give the world so much power that we paralyze our own mouths, we live as the wicked.

The wicked flee when no one pursues,
> but the righteous are as bold as a lion. (Proverbs 28:1)

This image from Proverbs is powerful. The wicked are trapped because they do not see clearly. They might look down a street, and though nothing is there to cause harm, they run, because in their mind they have constructed an elaborate scenario that promises doom. In the same way, as witnesses today, we often find ourselves out of breath, unable to open our mouths and quaking in fear because we think the world is pursuing us. But when we look back with wisdom, we see nothing. The threat lives only in our heads.

The righteous live with Jesus defining reality. We are committed to Jesus, and through his light we see clearly. We are as bold as lions.

One aspect of boldness in witness is being willing to discern true seekers after God from those who are mere hangers-on.

SEEKERS OR SNACKERS?

Jesus never wanted to be popular. His mission was to connect and commit people to the love of God. He wanted them set free by God's Word. So he delivered his words with power, challenge and comfort and then waited to see who would respond in faith. His goal wasn't massive crowds following him. In fact, after the crowds deserted him (as told in John 6), his brothers considered him such a failure that they put together a new recruitment plan (John 7:1-5). Jesus would have none of it. He wanted committed disciples following him, learning from him to deepen their experience of God's love.

Jesus' wisdom shines through in how he handled those who began to follow him. He closely monitored the effects of God's Word on the hearts and lives of people.

Our time, like Jesus', is limited. We could spend our whole lives confusing activity and accomplishment. We could be pouring all of our evangelistic resources and energy into the wrong people. Jesus was quick to understand who God was at work in and who he wasn't at work in. We, too, must learn to discern which of our friends are becoming genuine seekers and which are not.

Jesus had two camps of people: seekers and snackers. Do we?

Seekers are people who are genuine in their search for God. They are looking for something more in this world and they have a conviction that Jesus offers something special. They are willing to pay great costs to enter into new, spiritual culture, to come to church, to study the Word and to take real steps of faith toward God. These are the ones who will worship the Father in spirit and truth. Seekers have tasted something of God, and their lives have begun to manifest a deeper hunger for God himself.

Snackers are an entirely different type of person. The problem is that their actions and behaviors look very similar to those of seekers. Snackers are excited about being part of the spiritual "club" that is developing. They love it that Christians are servants, and they are eager for more chances to be served. They can never eat enough free, fresh-baked cookies. They might even find the Word of God somewhat interesting. But they do little to change their lives after hearing the Word of God. They look like seekers on the outside, but inside their hearts are wired completely differently.

Jesus had a harsh word for such snackers, according to John 6. He did not allow them to stay in their spiritual deception for long. He confronted them and called them to be true seekers. He publicly rebuked them for only coming for the bread that fed their stomachs. His immediate challenge for them was to become true seekers.

Like Christ, we must call our friends to become genuine seekers. They have to know that when they commit to Jesus, they are to live their lives based on God's priorities and not their own. This is a hard word today. Everyone wants to be "spiritual." Everyone wants to be liked. But everyone also wants an unaffected life, with Jesus' bread thrown in as a nice side dish. Few want to be true disciples.

Leading snackers into faith and commitment to Christ is a precarious venture. If snackers never become true seekers, they will likely fulfill Jesus' warning of people who "commit" but turn away when persecution and tribulation arise on account of the Word (Mark 4:16-17). These snackers never intended to change but instead saw Jesus as the spiritual appetizer-of-the-month. Jesus will never allow himself to be a side order for snackers; he wants to be their bread and water. And so we must make unbelievers see the true call of Christ.

The greatest temptation in relational witness is to stop at being relational. We can grow so comfortable with forming friendships with non-Christians that we forget that our purpose is to lead the skeptic into becoming a seeker and lead the seeker into becoming a disciple. If we are slow to challenge non-Christians in our GIGs, a new path begins to open up. It isn't the path that leads toward Jesus' school of discipleship; it is the path of spiritual fence-riding. The potential disciple becomes a snacker who hangs around and feels a part of things but will not commit to Christ.

Can you identify snackers in your witness ministry? If so, why have you been slow to lead them into deeper growth? A good place to start is to examine your own heart, as well as your need for training.

The path of evangelism is lined with many temptations. None of us has pure motives in evangelism. We are all tempted to define someone as a seeker because he or she has come to a Christian event. The snacker makes our witness ministry feel productive and somehow validates us. We are doing so much more than so-and-so over there! Jesus has a much purer joy for all of us than taking care of snackers so we feel better about ourselves.

Again, we must remember that Jesus never wanted to be popular. He wanted to set people free in the power of God's love. So we must ask why non-Christians are coming to our GIGs and our outreach events. And we must become skilled with God's Word to help them in the process of becoming genuine seekers. Do they really want Jesus, or are they hungry for our snacks?

Below are two accounts, one of a seeker and one of a snacker. I was a skeptic who became a seeker who became a disciple. My friend was a skeptic who became a snacker. My hope is that these two case studies will motivate us to help skeptics become seekers, and seekers full disciples of Jesus.

ON BECOMING A SEEKER

Angela and Derek sprinted down the hall at 3:30 in the morning, each spraying two cans of shaving cream at the other. By the time they reached the end of the floor, it looked like a light blue snow had fallen on the eighth floor of Dykstra Hall at UCLA. I enjoyed the moment as entertainment for the evening and wouldn't have given it another thought, but then I saw Dave come out of the bathroom.

Dave·Palmer was a Christian who lived on my dorm floor. He taught a Bible study and was always talking about Jesus. He once bought the floor a whole stack of pizzas to let us know about a Bible study. (I went into his meeting for five minutes, signed a fake name and strutted back to my dorm room with an entire pizza.) I wasn't interested in hearing about Jesus, but I was glad for the pizza. I was a flagrant snacker.

When Dave came out of the bathroom that night, he wore his fatigue like an overcoat. But after looking down our dorm hallway and sizing up the situation, he pivoted and went right back into the restroom. He quickly emerged from the bathroom with a stack of paper towels. He walked to the shaving cream, got on his hands and knees and began wiping the floor.

My friends and I were shocked. What was Dave doing? We knew he was religious, but this was ridiculous. We went for a closer look. As we peered over his shoulder, he continued his work. I cleared my throat and asked him, "Dave, why are you cleaning the hallway?"

He stopped wiping, looked up at me and said, "Because Jesus would." He returned to cleaning.

I quickly tapped him on the shoulder to ask him my next question. "Dave, why would Jesus clean a dorm floor at four in the morning?"

He stopped, looked me in the eye again and replied, "Because Jesus is a servant." He returned to his cleaning, inching farther down the hall.

I was drawn in by Dave's short but striking answers. So I approached Dave for the third and final time. "Dave, why would Jesus clean the floor at four in the morning? The maid is coming in a few hours. Why wouldn't he let her do her job?"

He looked up again and this time spoke directly into my soul. "John, Jesus, being God, has all of his needs met, so he puts himself beneath everyone. He loves caring for those on the bottom. He loves the maid who cleans this hallway. I am only living out his love for her."

His answer confused me at first. But on a soul level I realized that I had no idea who Jesus was. If I were asked to describe Jesus, the word *servant* would not have been in my top one hundred. The description "spiritual cop" would have been near the top. But Dave was so captivated by Jesus' servant love that he lived it out. Even at four o'clock in the morning.

I didn't know what exactly was happening, but something spiritual and special was going on for me. My friends and I joined Dave and began to wipe up shaving cream. Afterward, Dave invited me to his GIG.

I ended up going to Dave's GIG faithfully for the rest of the year. Dave taught me God's Word and he answered my questions. I took real steps of faith in prayer, love for the poor and reconciliation of broken relationships. I saw Jesus come through for me. I began attending the larger Christian community events. I loved worship and I began to hunger for God's Word. The Word had engaged me. I was slowly being pulled out of the world. I had become a seeker.

After six months of growth by learning to pray and by applying God's Word to my alcohol struggles, broken relationships and anxieties over my studies, I became a Christian. My conversion was solid because it was already rooted in God's Word. My final decision for Christ was the conclusion, not the beginning, of my seeking process.

After three years of further training and development, I became a campus minister. I have now been on staff with IVCF for seven years. I was ignorant, but I received a taste of Jesus' bread and was finally taught to feed on the Bread of Life himself.

STUCK IN SNACKERVILLE

Michael lived on the dorm floor where a handful of Christian leaders had committed to reaching out to younger students and non-Christians. He came from a highly secular background and liked poking fun at Christians. Yet he came to our Bible study and enjoyed being around us. He particularly liked one of the Christian student leaders. He thought she was cute.

During the next nine months, Michael became a regular part of our lives. A *very* regular part. About five of us ministered to him. We would stay up at night answering his questions. We would go out of our way to care for him and bless him. We cooked for him, helped him with his laundry, let him borrow our cars, loaned him money. I even took him on weekend getaways with my friends. All of us thought that the next act of service, the next conversation or the next Bible study would be the one that would cause Michael to follow Christ. Unfortunately that next step never came. He regularly told us that he needed God to do a miracle in his life before he would believe. When a miracle would in fact happen, he would come up with a new reason not to commit.

I wish I knew then about Jesus' teachings on seekers and snackers. I wish I had had my own philosophy about how to identify seekers and snackers over the course of six months. Instead I blindly committed to Michael all of my time and resources. And he was the most classic snacker I have ever met. Why *wouldn't* the guy like Christians? We were like a personal maid service for him. Of course he liked us, but he would never become one of us. What Michael needed was an honest challenge to begin seeking the true bread from heaven. Instead we kept feeding him the bread that perishes. And in effect, five student ministers spent the bulk of an academic year pouring our spiritual energy, prayer, money and time into a snacker. We had been duped by the world.

Over and over again I have seen relational witnesses snared in the trap of becoming "best friends" with non-Christians who are being dishonest about their spiritual search. We must call on God for courage to have conversations that call forth the motives of snackers. Jesus was honest and firm with the crowd who came for wrong reasons. If we do not challenge such people to take genuine steps toward God and work through their blocks to faith, we will never know what is going on inside of their souls. On the outside they look like faithful seekers, but inside they are hungry for relationships, a place to belong, emotional healing, money, time, attention—anything and everything except the Bread of Life. We must discern what true spiritual growth looks like in people's lives, for if we do not, we will assume the best in them and waste our most precious evangelism resource—time.

In the end, it is not a good investment for witnesses to spend countless hours building trust, serving and teaching the Word to people who have no desire to change. Yes, we are "planting seeds." But we would all agree that planting seeds on concrete is not a good investment of seed. Life is too short to spend it all on snackers.

Jesus does not play games when it comes to the world. He was not afraid of the world and he gave it little power over him because he didn't want popularity. He knew people and what was in their hearts. And he had compassion, so he taught the Word. He called forth the seekers. He challenged the snackers. Jesus kept his witness real.

KEY CONCEPTS

Jesus' handling of the world

- He had compassion on both spiritually needy and spiritually arrogant people, teaching them the gospel.
- Do we view the world as a Goliath or a moldable lump of clay?

Jesus' handling of the world with his Word

- Today people must be taught the basics of the Bible.
- They are more open than we might think to learning the Bible.
- Jesus gave people an experience of his Word and monitored their reactions to him.

Seekers or snackers?

- Seekers are people who are helped into genuinely seeking God.
- Snackers are people who hang around for Christian blessings.
- We must challenge people earlier to discern if they are truly open.

GROWTH STEP

Reflect on one of your non-Christian evangelistic relationships, then answer the following questions.

1. How has your non-Christian friend responded to the Word lived out or to invitations to the GIG?
2. On a scale of one to ten, what is the person's passion for the Word?
3. How might you challenge the person to see whether he or she is really open to living in God?
4. How has the person been challenged to pray?
5. How has the person been challenged to repent and experience the joy of obedience?
6. What are you learning about Jesus from ministering to this person?
7. What have you learned about yourself as you have urged this person on in his or her faith?

FIVE

SENT
BY GOD

*The Father who sent me has himself testified on my behalf.
. . . You do not have his word abiding in you,
because you do not believe him whom he has sent.*

JESUS OF NAZARETH

*Hope means a continual looking forward to the eternal world.
It does not mean that we are to leave the present world as it is.
If you read history you will find that the Christians who did most for the
present world were just those who thought most of the next.*

C. S. LEWIS

The UCLA basketball team won the national championship in 1995. It had been twenty years since my alma mater had raised a title banner. I followed the team every step of the way, even sleeping outside the basketball arena to secure courtside seats reserved for students. The title run was full of drama, and the whole campus celebrated the triumph.

Our InterVarsity community of faith wanted to be part of the campus celebration, so we hosted a party. We cooked great food, spun great CDs and, at my suggestion, decorated my apartment to resemble UCLA's basketball court. We hung eleven title banners around the room, pinned a hoop to the wall and even taped the carpet to look like the lines on a basketball court. We used masking tape. That turned out to be a bad idea.

Bad things happen when three hundred college students dance, sweat, stomp, fall and spill drinks on masking-taped carpet for five hours. Very bad things. After the party, I realized just how bad an idea it was. The tape wouldn't come up. It had been ground into the carpet so thoroughly that it was difficult to know where the carpet ended and the tape began. On my hands and knees, after ten minutes of digging into the carpet for tape, I had pulled up only small flecks of tape. My heart sank when I calculated how long this was going to take. It was going to be a long night.

I continued to labor next to TinaLee, who was part of the clean-up team. Her nails were longer than mine and she was able to dig deeper to remove the tape from the carpet. As we worked, someone came to me and told me that I needed to check on another catastrophe in a different part of my apartment. I told Tina I would be right back.

I returned fifteen minutes later. The tape-digging crew was hard at work, though their attitude was beginning to resemble that of the Israelites when they were told to make more bricks for Pharaoh. They questioned what rocket scientist came up with the tape-on-the-carpet idea. I pretended not to hear them, took a deep breath and went back down on my knees.

To my surprise, as I put my fingers under the tape, I found I had a grip. I began to pull the tape. It just kept coming up. And coming. And coming! The tape was seemingly moving at the speed of light, and it didn't stop for about ten inches. I couldn't believe my luck. I thrust my hands in the air as though I had just won UCLA the title. I was just about to tell everyone I had discovered the breakthrough we were all waiting for when I saw Tina's face. Her smile was even bigger than mine.

While I was gone, Tina had done all the hard work of pulling up the tape. Her nails reached what I could not reach and she pulled up

tape I could not pull up. She then placed it back down, leaving it as
a treasure for me to discover. In other words, she did all the real work,
leaving me the thrill of pulling tape.

APPLAUSE AND JOY

God the Father is committed to winning the world through witness
and invites us into his labor. A psalmist described God as the One
who never sleeps nor slumbers (Psalm 121:4). Jesus told us that his Father is always working (John 5:17). Winning the world is his job. We
are sent by him to deliver a witness so that all might believe.

Witnesses do not make decisions for people. We cannot change
hearts. We pray, give evidence, connect the dots, teach the Word,
testify to the truth, persuade, compel and beg. But we never decide
for another. The decision to obey God or not obey God is always
between the person and God. And it is God, with the precision of
a surgeon, who cuts into the hearts and lives of people with circumstances, relationships, longings, pain and supernatural communication to convince them to put their hope in him. God, in his
sovereign love, makes sinners come alive by giving them new life
in the Spirit. "To all who received him, who believed in his name,
he gave power to become children of God, who were born, not of
blood or of the will of the flesh or of the will of man, but of God"
(John 1:12-13).

It is good news that, as we get the word out, we are going where
God has already been. God knows that we are overmatched in our
task of calling the world to follow Jesus. So he goes before us, wins
the spiritual battles in the hearts of humans and invites us to share in
his victory. God receives the credit, the honor and the fame. We receive the joy. He is the Father who loves to give good gifts to his children. And to his witnesses.

This picture of God does not ignore the day-to-day challenges
of being a witness. I agree with Winston Churchill, who wrote in

The Hinge of Fate that the greatest mistake a leader can make is to fill people with a false hope that is soon swept away. So let me say this again: evangelism is difficult. Leading people through the sometimes long and pain-filled process of conversion will often not feel like my joy in pulling tape. Many will reject the message, even making false accusations and cursing us as we try to bless. Yet that expected reaction from the world should never cause us to feel that God does not lead us to where he is already at work. Instead, the rejection, indifference and disappointment should tell us that God has not yet chosen to dig up that particular piece of tape. But he is always working.

Seeing God as the One who sends us out as witnesses forces us to be hopeful. Hope is one of the most underrated qualities in evangelism. For one thing, what non-Christian would want to heed the message of a hopeless person? We must be the message that we bring. The hopeless witness will also miss many doors that the Lord opens. J. Robert Clinton defines hope as walking down the street and believing something really good is right around the corner. Hopeless witnesses will not walk through an open door in faith; they will walk right past it with their heads down. Seeing God as the worker who goes before us forces us to walk through life with our heads up. It forces us to live as though he has already been drawing people to himself. Thus we will investigate the lives of our friends more closely, looking for God's fingerprints. We will ask questions with greater wisdom and clarity. We will teach the Scripture with greater authority and boldness. We will call for commitment with greater confidence and urgency.

How we view God makes all the difference in our evangelism. We will no longer be surprised to discover that our friend is interested in God. We would do well to assume that our friend *is* interested, because the Father has already been there. Saving sinners is at the very center of the heart of God! His great mission is what he sends us into.

MERCY-FILLED DEPLOYMENT

Sending witnesses is one of the great acts of God. "His predominant 'character'-istic is that he sent Jesus," says Alan Culpepper in *The Anatomy of the Fourth Gospel*. "Sending characterizes God's self-revelation."

Just as in our present-day world, where business leaders and political leaders send their best people to represent them in great matters, so it is with God and the spiritual world. The living One, the most powerful and awesome person in the universe, sends his people to represent him and to fulfill his purposes on the earth. As he monitors all activities from the great throne of the universe, he is in close contact with those he sends as the kingdom of God breaks into the earth. God has been sending his people from the beginning.

God sent Abraham from Ur in Chaldea to a land that he would show him so that Abraham could take his place in God's plan of redemptive history. "The LORD said to Abram, 'Go from your country and your kindred and your father's house to the land that I will show you. I will make of you a great nation, and I will bless you, and make your name great, so that you will be a blessing" (Genesis 12:1-2).

God sent Moses to Pharaoh so that he could free the people of Israel. God said, "Come, I will send you to Pharaoh to bring my people, the Israelites, out of Egypt" (Exodus 3:10).

God sent the prophet Isaiah to speak his word to the children of Israel. Isaiah testified, "I heard the voice of the Lord saying, 'Whom shall I send, and who will go for us?' And I said, 'Here am I; send me!'" (Isaiah 6:8).

God sent the prophet Jeremiah to be a prophet for all the nations. Jeremiah recalled,

> Now the word of the LORD came to me saying,
> "Before I formed you in the womb I knew you,
> and before you were born I consecrated you;
> I appointed you a prophet to the nations."

Then I said, "Ah, Lord GOD! Truly I do not know how to speak, for I am only a boy." But the LORD said to me,

"Do not say, 'I am only a boy';
for you shall go to all to whom I send you,
and you shall speak whatever I command you.
Do not be afraid of them." (Jeremiah 1:4-8)

Sending is one of the great mercies of God. As God sends his people to proclaim his message, his purposes mean life for those who love him. Just as large pharmaceutical companies make the decision to send supplies that can save thousands of lives to countries in need around the globe, so the decision of God to send his people will result in life to those who embrace his message. The sent one is the physical representative of God's love and his personal commitment to ensuring the good and happy future of those who put their hope in him. The person sent by God embodies God's own promise to make his face shine on his people. Sending is not the beginning of a process. It is the culmination. It is the application and resource allocation. It is deployment—mercy-filled deployment!

Being sent is a major theme of the Fourth Gospel. The apostle John uses the Greek word for "sending" sixty-three times. The Father is referred to in various forms as "the one who sent" twenty-three times, seventeen of those times in relation to his sending Jesus. Being sent was the authority base that Jesus claimed in every interaction where he was challenged by the religious leaders. The theme is introduced in the prologue with John the Baptist's description as being sent by God for witness. And from the moment Jesus emerged as a public leader, he showed us what it means to live sent. He lived in the fullness of God's authority, the power that is unmatched in all the earth, and with the focus and urgency that the mission required.

How could the disciples know what Jesus meant when he said the

Father had sent him? They would only have to remember what they saw with their own eyes. They saw Jesus skillfully and thoughtfully calling new people to follow God. That is what it means to be sent by God. They saw him going through the temple, turning over the tables of injustice to establish God's community. That is what it means to be sent by God. They saw Jesus demonstrate the power of God by turning water into wine, healing lame people, feeding thousands of people with five barley loaves and even calling forth life from the grave. That is what Jesus understood his mission to be when he was sent by God. His Father gave him everything he needed to fulfill that mission. He then sent his disciples, giving them everything they needed.

BREATHING ON ORDINARY PEOPLE

Jesus was sent to send. But was he certain about who he was sending? Didn't the Lord keep up with current events? In John 20 we see that the disciples were not doing well. Peter had betrayed Jesus and would have to live with the guilt and shame of that experience. The others, like Peter, had just fled from danger to leave Jesus to die alone on the cross. They were hiding out in a safe house because they were afraid they would be captured and killed, just as Jesus was killed. These scared and emotionally fragile men were the witnesses Jesus chose to send. If you and I were on Jesus' ministry board or served as his consultant, we might have wanted to have a word with him before this dramatic commissioning ceremony, to double-check why he was sending this group.

I believe that we are to be deeply encouraged by who Jesus sends. He does not send people who have no problems. He does not send disciples who long for more suffering and conflict. He does not send people who have proven time and again they can handle the pressure. He sends ordinary people who are trying their best to love God. The commission to be sent for witness must have been surreal for this ragtag bunch of disciples. It is like a team of rookies being elevated to all-star status. The spotlight was suddenly on them, and they were pointing at themselves, saying, "Who, us?"

Hearing Jesus' words, their minds surely flooded with memories from the last three years. Could they do what Jesus did? They couldn't even go out for a newspaper at this point; how were they going to live sent? They probably wanted to scream out that Jesus was sending the wrong folks. But in reality they were perfect candidates for being sent. I like John Piper's observation in his sermon "Brother, Tell Them Not to Serve God!" that Jesus differs from Uncle Sam because the soldier in Uncle Sam's army must be perfectly healthy, while the soldier in Jesus' army must be spiritually sick.

Jesus' call and commission to live sent are not merely words. Being sent is a call that is to be empowered by God. We cannot live in our human power. We need supernatural help. Jesus did not give his disciples a motivational speech about what a great witness their inner child was. He didn't try to frame their current failures as a "witness slump." Jesus knew he was leading them into an impossible task—impossible, that is, unless they would be connected with God in the same way he was. He knew they were scared, weak and overwhelmed. So he breathed on them and told them to "receive the Holy Spirit" (John 20:22).

Jesus' words and actions take us back to Genesis 2:7, where we read how God breathed life into the first man. Before the breath of God, Adam was merely a mud figure. After receiving God's breath, he became alive.

Jesus' breath also leads us back to Ezekiel 37. The prophet was shown a valley of dry bones that formed a massive grave site that must have churned his stomach. Ezekiel gave words of prophecy over the valley, and immediately bone, sinew, flesh and skin grew together. But the reconstituted bodies were still not alive. God then sent his breath, and the dry bones miraculously came together, an army of the Lord.

In the same way, before Jesus breathed on them, the disciples were lifeless mud and a dead army. They were not alive for witness. They did not have the power of the Holy Spirit. After Jesus breathed the Spirit into them, however, they became an exceedingly great army of witnesses. These men would carry Jesus' message to the ends of the earth.

When Jesus sends his witnesses, he sends us with power to fulfill our divine purpose!

SENT FOR A PURPOSE

In our day-to-day lives, when we are sent, we are given specific tasks to accomplish. My mom will not send me to the store just to send me to the store; she will send me to the store for milk or for cookies. When our parents send us to college, the goal is to return with a degree. When our boss sends us to enter into negotiations on a deal, we are supposed to bring back a signed contract.

Recently my wife and I decided to remodel a room in our home. My friend Doug Ribbens, a gifted builder, graciously volunteered to organize the project. During Doug's first walk-through of the room, I could almost hear his mind processing the possibilities as he looked with his experienced, trained eyes. He quickly sketched out what the room might become on his legal pad. Then he sent me to Home Depot with a detailed list of the resources we would need for the project. He told me which products and brands to purchase and which to avoid.

I wrote down every word from Doug's mouth. I didn't want to be like all the other weekend builders who end up going to Home Depot seven times in a weekend. I even borrowed the store phone to call him multiple times from the store to make sure I was picking up the right materials.

I went to Home Depot with my list in hand. I was sent by Doug to be a part of his larger plan. In the same way, God has a specific plan for sending us that is a part of his larger plans. This is what we must remember when things get tough.

Living as a witness is not welcomed in many places in this world. In some locations there are steep costs to being a witness; in others, the restrictions are of a more social nature. But as we are sent, we must know that God creates a place for us. Those of us from shame-based cultures, in particular, need to realize that we are not bringing shame on ourselves or our family as we proclaim the gospel. In fact, it is just the opposite. We are bringing honor to our family name. We will be honored by God, the highest authority of all.

Though it can be difficult to live as though God has sent us with direction and purpose, we need not wander or fear shame. We have a role to fill. We are sent for witness. Those are our papers. That is our place in the world. We will surely be *more than* a witness in our lifetime—we will be mothers, fathers, wives, husbands, teachers, firefighters, professors, doctors, missionaries, whatever—but we can never be *less than* a witness.

Being sent from God forever changed the life of each disciple in Jesus' little band. Discipleship became their identity and affected every detail of their lives. Being sent should also change our lives.

We would do well to embrace the identity in God that Jesus embraced. Being sent was how Jesus defined himself. What keeps us from defining ourselves in a similar way? If we understand ourselves to be sent, we will set ourselves firmly on the foundation built by the prophets, apostles and great men and women whom God has used to change the world. We will access a spiritual identity that rises above the wrecking balls of criticism and rejection. We will enjoy sweeter communion with the One who sends us as we come to him with our every need, dream and hope. And when we take ourselves more seriously, we will see the world differently. We will see the tape that God has laid for us to lift. We will walk with hope into the darkest of situations. We will speak and teach Jesus' words of hope.

THE GREAT TEMPTATION— SENDING OURSELVES

As we accept our identity as witnesses, one of the great temptations we will face is that of not going to the ones to whom God sends us. We often make our own decisions about who God is at work in (as though there were any we could know with no personal investigation). Certainly we will make decisions about who God sends us to. And we will more times than not choose the people we feel comfortable with. In doing so, we will miss much of the work that God has already done. Let's remember: we never send ourselves.

I met William my first week of planting a new InterVarsity chapter at Cal State Dominguez Hills. He was a senior, and I could quickly tell that people respected him. He had what you might call a healthy self-image. As I met him, I told him I was the new campus pastor, and I asked him what he would do if he were starting a new community of faith at DH. I secretly hoped he would first comment on the half-smoked marijuana cigarette that was falling out of his sock, but he chose to answer my question.

He put his hand on my shoulder and confidently told me that I need to go to the people who are open to God. I thought that was sound advice. He then publicly, and loudly, pointed at a young man who was kissing his girlfriend under a tree. The couple was no more than ten feet from us, but William could not have cared less and began yelling, "Do you see that guy? Look at him. He is getting his romance on. He is getting on his macaroni. He doesn't care about God. Don't go after that guy. There is no way he would be interested in God."

Before I could even laugh at how wild this experience had quickly become, he whirled me around and pointed out another student walking up the sidewalk. This guy wore glasses, he was under round-the-clock surveillance by the fashion police, and he looked like he studied fifty hours a week purely for pleasure. William excitedly began pointing him out. "That's him, right there. Dawg, that's him! That is the guy you want to invite. He would be open to God."

At first I chuckled at William's spiritual naiveté. I was the missionary. How silly to assume that you can tell the inner workings of God in people's lives based on just looking at them! Right in the middle of my laugh, though, God began to turn that laugh in my own direction. I was convicted that I do the same thing all the time. I thought of all the unspoken yet decisive judgments I make, in the quickness of a second, deciding whether or not people are open to God. How ludicrous to think we can see inside someone's soul! How equally ludicrous to assume chess players are more open to the gospel than young Casanovas! What would William have thought about the young apostle Paul? The great apostle would have been overlooked immediately.

The sent witness should never ask, who is open to God? When we go down that road, we will invariably minister to those we are most comfortable with. Instead we should ask who God is sending us to. Who is God already at work in, making them ready for harvest? Those are the people who are open to God. And the last time I checked my Bible and my ministry experiences, God digs deep into the lives of people you and I would never have guessed in a hundred years. The stakes are too high to miss the opportunities God sets before us. Living sent will cause us to reach out to people we might be uncomfortable with.

GARY MOTON

I had much fear in my heart my first day at Dominguez Hills. As I drove to campus, my mind was swirling with dark scenarios. What would my first day be like? I had never started a community of faith from scratch. I was so different from most everyone on the campus. As a biracial Korean European on a majority black and Latino campus, would I be liked? Would anyone be interested in the gospel? My stomach felt like I had eaten eight pieces of pizza for breakfast. And then threw down some coffee.

That morning I soberly asked Jesus to help me believe he had sent me to DH. I told him I needed to see a sign that day to help me believe he was the one starting a new ministry. I begged him to breathe on me. I needed all the help I could get. I parked my car, took a deep breath and began the long and lonely walk toward the middle of my new campus.

The first hour did not go well. Everyone I spoke to blew me off. I moved from group to group, and no one wanted me around. I was beginning to doubt my sentness. I went into the bathroom, splashed some water on my face, took a few more deep breaths and went down to get some lunch.

As I entered the campus eatery, I began to look around the room. I immediately saw a young man who seemed to have a soft glow about him. I did a double take. I looked a third time, pinched myself and almost audibly mouthed, "Yes, that guy does seem to have a light around him." God had never spoken to me in this way before, but I had been told by a mentor to be ready for "divine appointments" when planting a new ministry. I assumed the "glow" I saw indicated this was one of those divine appointments.

I walked toward the young man's table. Eating his lunch, he looked as if he wasn't interested in company. But I took another deep breath and introduced myself. "Hi, my name is John. This is my first day at DH. Can I eat lunch with you?"

He looked up at me and his countenance softened. He replied, "This is my first day too. I am a freshman. Yeah, please sit down."

We shared small talk for ten minutes, and then I began to seek why

God was sending me to Gary. We were talking about high school, so I decided to be vulnerable with him. I wanted to fish a little bit and see if he would bite on the spiritual bait I was throwing out.

"Gary, the thing I regret most about high school was how destructive I was. I really messed myself up. I was dealing with emotional pain from a family tragedy and I couldn't deal with my pain. I ended up doing crazy things. I hurt my family and my own soul."

Gary immediately connected with my experience and began to share his own pain. "John, that's nothing. My father left when I was one, and my mother has been abusive with me since I can remember. I have a lot of anger inside of me."

Having confessed how I dealt with my issues, I asked how he dealt with his stuff. He told me that he had many coping mechanisms, but the most destructive of all was fire. I leaned over because I was sure I had misheard him. "What was that?"

"Fire, John, fire. I dealt with my stuff by trying to burn things down. I once burned down a field. I liked the feeling of controlling the burn."

I was shocked when I realized that God had sent me to a potential arsonist. But I know that when athletes are in pressure situations they are told, "Act like you have been there before." So I pretended like I had heard struggles with self-control and fire a million times and nodded to keep the conversation flowing normally. He assured me that he hadn't struggled with fire issues for years. He must have seen me shift in my seat and wanted to make me feel more comfortable.

I continued to see if he would go to the God level with me. "Gary, I wish when I was in high school I would have known what I know now. I have found an amazing way to deal with my own grief, pain, loss and fear. I know this might sound weird, but God helps me with all my problems."

Gary said it didn't sound weird to him, but he quickly noted that his experience of religion had not been positive. "John, when I was young, my grandmother was really religious. I actually liked God and I really liked learning about the Bible. But she would go to church on Saturdays and make me go all day long with her. I wanted to play baseball and do sports on Saturday. She said that God didn't like sports and made me go with her. What kind of God wouldn't let me play baseball on Saturday?"

When Gary said that, he touched a chord deep inside me. I assured him that the God I know would have wanted him to play baseball when he was a boy. I told him that the God I know is entirely committed to making his people happy. Gary thought that was pretty cool.

I made my next move. "Gary, I am starting a Christian fellowship on this campus. I love teaching the Bible to people who have had bad experiences with church. I have these studies that I call GIGs. You learn the Bible for yourself, ask any questions you want and, best of all, there are no churchgoing Christians allowed. I would love for you to get to know the God I know. Would you be up for getting together?"

Gary thought about it for a minute and said, "John, I like your new religion. Yeah, I would love to get together with you for a GIG. How about tomorrow?"

I laughed under my breath and thought about what my ministry partners might think if they heard I was starting a new religion. I nailed down a time to meet with Gary. We began our GIG the next day.

During that first month of GIGs, with much prayer and many meals, God moved powerfully into the center of Gary's life. He became a Christian and joined our IVCF community of faith, More Than Conquerors, at Dominguez Hills. Since his conversion, his life has changed dramatically. He actively repented of the sins that were keeping him down. He has worked out many issues with his mother and stepfather. He has a voracious appetite for God's Word. His friends even gave him a nickname, "The Deacon," because during our study on one of our retreats he couldn't contain his excitement over the Word and started emphatically preaching for five minutes.

The rest of the students egged him on, "Preach, Deacon, preach!" Gary told us this was the first time he had ever had a nickname.

THE JOY OF ACCOMPLISHING GOD'S PURPOSES

God sent me to Gary. He had a plan and purpose all along. He knew I would meet Gary while I was driving to campus with a thousand butterflies in my stomach. He answered my prayers for more of the Holy Spirit. Jesus heard my cries and breathed on me. He sent me to Gary that first day because he knew I needed to deepen my faith to start a new ministry. God sent me for witness to DH so that Gary and many others like him would become people who worship Jesus.

Each person you meet could be a piece of tape that God has placed just for you. You might be the key to that person's next step toward the kingdom of God. Whether you are planting a seed or reaping a great harvest, the tape awaits you. How many people has God placed before us that we have walked right by, not knowing he has been there, working in their soul? The answer is too many. Please don't pull a William and assume you know who God has been working in. Inhale Jesus' breath of life and live sent!

KEY CONCEPTS

The Father goes before us

- We should assume that God is at work in our friends' lives.
- Witnesses strive to discover how God is already at work.
- He does the spiritual work we can't do, and invites us into his victory.
- Witnesses who believe God is at work will be full of hope.

Jesus sends us

- Just as Jesus was sent by the Father, so he sends us, his disciples.
- The disciples were feeble when they were sent.
- Jesus' breath equips us all to live sent for witness in this world.

Sent by God or ourselves?

- We cannot tell by externals who God is at work in; we must dig.
- The question should never be, who is open to the gospel?
- The question should be, who is God at work in?
- Each person you meet could be a piece of tape placed by God.
- There is no greater joy than being a part of someone's conversion.

GROWTH STEP

Think of one or two of your non-Christian friends.

1. What will you do to deepen the reality that Jesus personally sends you to your friends for witness?
2. How does that change the way you view your friendships?
3. How is God already at work in their lives?
4. Are they going through pain?
5. Did they formerly know God?
6. Do they have a curiosity for the Word? (If you are not sure, you should probably get a little closer and do some more digging.)

SIX

FILLED WITH
THE SPIRIT

The Spirit of God comes into us to fill us with his passion
to see the Father and the Son glorified.

DARRELL JOHNSON

I met Colossus the first day we started the IVCF More Than Conquerors ministry at Compton Community College. He was without question the most physically intimidating student I had ever met. He stood around 6 feet tall and weighed in at around 280 pounds. He had muscles upon his muscles, spoke with a deep, pounding voice and carried himself like a wrestler. (I later found out he made it to the final rounds of professional wrestling tryouts on MTV.)

During the first couple of days, we got to know each other and connected over sports, his love life and daily life in Compton. I wanted to introduce him to Jesus, so I invited him to a GIG. He said he was up for it and even added that he wanted to see what Jesus was like. So we studied the sign of Jesus turning water into wine. Colossus really liked it. He found Jesus to be down-to-earth yet full of power. He said that he was the kind of person you would definitely want to invite to your party.

My central goal as a GIG leader is that people will leave God's Word having met God's Son and having personally invited him into a need, struggle or situation so that they can experience God getting involved in their life. So as we moved into the application time of our

GIG, I asked Colossus to identify an area of his life where he felt "like he had run out of wine." He quickly identified the thirsty area. I shared with him mine and told him that I needed Jesus that day as much as he did. I suggested we then pray for God's love and power to move in our lives, and I asked if he was comfortable to begin praying. He said he was.

He began with words that almost made me choke on my gum. "O great Odin! This is your servant warrior Colossus."

I quickly looked up, shook my head (because my ears must have been clogged) and asked him, "What did you say?"

"I began praying like you asked me to, John."

"Who did you pray to?"

"Odin."

"Who is Odin?"

"He is the Norse god of war. Me and my friends are into witchcraft. We're really into Odin right now."

At that point I didn't know what to do. I had never seen anyone pray to a false god at the end of a Bible study. InterVarsity never trained me for this one. I silently prayed under my breath and asked the Holy Spirit for help. As I sat in God's presence, I felt a rush of confidence in God. I felt like God was telling me to challenge Colossus and not let him finish our time in John 2 with a prayer to Odin.

"Colossus, I know that you are checking out Odin and all, but I want you to focus on Jesus right now. We just studied about how he turned water into wine. He wants to do the same thing for you. Right now. I want you to pray to Jesus and tell him what you need."

Colossus looked up at me, thought about it and agreed. He told Jesus about where the wine was out in his life and invited Jesus to help him with his need.

Jesus moved powerfully in Colossus's life that semester. We continued our GIG for about seven weeks. Colossus had big questions about the Trinity, God's real name, professional wrestling and how to deal with his anger. Through his attending our GIGs and forming deep friendships with our fledgling IVCF community, he experienced more and more of God's love. In a genuine step of faith, Colossus asked Jesus for a wondrous sign about the future so that he could know Jesus was real. God answered that sign for Colossus in a way that made Jesus look really good! Colossus responded to God's sign by attending an IVCF conference. That weekend he and his two friends became followers of Jesus. Colossus no longer puts his hope in Odin or other gods. Shortly after Colossus's conversion, God had put new words in his mouth: "O great Yahweh, this is Colossus, your servant warrior."

If you were to tell me three years ago that I would be ministering to semiprofessional wrestlers in Compton, I would have told you that you were crazy. But God's Spirit empowers us to do things we cannot do. Or would not naturally choose to do. It is the Spirit of God dwelling in us who leads us into situations where he must work his ministry. He gets the credit and we get the joy. As God sends us, he gives us what we need to give Jesus' life to others. Even people who pray to Norse gods.

THE MINISTRY OF THE HOLY SPIRIT

The apostle John had at least thirty years of experience with the Holy Spirit before he penned the Fourth Gospel. He was personally used by the Spirit to make a lame man walk (Acts 3:1-10). He anointed young believers in Samaria to receive God's Spirit (Acts 8:14-17). He preached, evangelized and led in the power of the Spirit for decades. Consequently, John, of all the Gospel authors, was by far the best equipped to deliver teaching on the nature and ministry of the Holy Spirit. Oh, that we may know what John knew!

> He whom God has sent speaks the words of God, for he gives the Spirit without measure. The Father loves the Son and has placed all things into his hands. (John 3:34-35)

I tell you the truth: it is to your advantage that I go away, for
if I do not go away, the Advocate will not come to you; but if
I go, I will send him to you. And when he comes, he will
prove the world wrong about sin and righteousness and judgment. (John 16:7-8)

In John 20 we read how the disciples were helplessly overmatched
against all the internal and external enemies of witness. With the
Spirit of God, though, they were empowered and equipped to lead
the world to faith. But what exactly is the ministry of the Holy Spirit?
What did the disciples receive when Jesus breathed on them? John 3
and John 16 shed light on the ministry of the Holy Spirit.

John 3:34 teaches that the one whom God has sent speaks the
words of God. This sharpens our understanding of what it means to
live sent. The main function of the one sent by God is to speak his
words. We get the word out because the words of Jesus contain eternal life, and the Spirit is committed to getting the word out. As the
words go out, there is life inside them. They are like smart bombs
that will explode in their designated time. The key is getting the
smart bombs to their proper destination. Because there is unearthly
power in Jesus' words, they must be spoken.

Yes, we are sent to pray, serve, care for others and be a model of
holiness. But John 3 defines the ones who are sent by God as the people who will speak the words of God in the world. We can pray until
our knees are worn, serve until our bones break and live with more
integrity than any other human on the planet, but until we open our
mouths to speak God's words, the gospel will not impact the lives of
our friends. People come to faith by hearing and understanding the
words of life.

The logical connector "for" in verse 34 sheds further light on why
and how the sent ones speak the word of God. The text teaches us
that the sent person speaks the words of life because the Father gives

the Spirit without measure. When I first studied this magnificent promise from God, my heart leaped within my body. This verse should liberate us to no end. Sent ones do not speak the word because they are tanks who could not care less about what others think. Nor do they open their mouths because they are full of guilt and need to check off the evangelism box on their Christian duty list. The power to speak the word of God does not come from us; it comes from God. Sent ones speak the word because God gives them the Spirit.

The Holy Spirit inside believers overrides our natural senses so that we will do what is fundamentally unnatural for us. It is not natural to witness to the world about Jesus. That is why we need the Spirit to be given to us, every day, without limit. The Spirit's ministry is to open our souls, our eyes, our minds and most importantly our mouths so that we can teach people to see the invisible God. When the Spirit comes to live inside us, he is committed to getting Jesus "out" through us. We cannot get the word out on our own. We are able to speak the words of God only because he gives us the Spirit. Witness is not about us; it is about Jesus breathing on us and into us through his Holy Spirit.

Jesus, in the upper-room meal, gave the disciples a new paradigm for looking at his imminent departure (John 16:7). He told them that they should be happy he was leaving, because when he left, he would send them his Holy Spirit. The Spirit is the one who convicts the world of sin. He is the one who stirs the conscience of individuals so that they might see themselves as sinners. He is the grace of God to help helpless sinners see what is true and not what is false. His work is to work on the hearts, minds and consciences of people, to cause them to understand the law of God and help them seek to obey it.

I enjoy watching the television show *Law & Order*. The second half of the show features articulate, prepared and persuasive district attorneys working hard for the conviction. The lawyers are masterful as they dig deep to uncover the truth, break down hard witnesses and reveal concise and convicting evidence that comes to reveal the truth. But more masterful than they, the Spirit of God is the greatest Counselor of all. When he speaks, no one can deny his truth. His words are able to penetrate the most fortressed heart. While the motives of the district attorney on *Law & Order* are for justice, God's Spirit convicts the world of sin out of love. It is his love for sinners that drives him to cause them to repent.

Without the ministry of the Holy Spirit, our friends would not repent. That is why Jesus taught the disciples that they should welcome the Spirit with open arms. That is why it was actually much better for them that he leave.

HOW MUCH GOD CAN WE HANDLE?

The question is never, does God wants us to be witnesses? Yahweh speaks powerfully that his people *are* his witnesses (Isaiah 43:10). The Holy Spirit abiding in us equips every believer to be a witness. The question is, will we say yes to God's plan to develop us into witnesses? Will we create inside our souls a home for the Holy Spirit so that he can perform his ministry of speaking God's words through us? God wants this for the world and for us. Will we say yes to Jesus and receive the Holy Spirit?

How much of the Holy Spirit can you handle? How much of his evangelism ministry do you wish to experience?

The apostle John was compelled to help us understand how much God wants the Holy Spirit to lead us and direct us in our witness. He most likely knew that we would find some reason to act as if this amazing promise did not apply to us. Will God give me enough of the Holy Spirit to make me a witness? Does he know how hard it is for me to open my mouth? God knows our weakness.

Therefore, God gives the Holy Spirit without measure to his sent ones. His giving is boundless, immeasurable and unending. Is that not the theme of Jesus' previous teachings about the Spirit in John? He proclaimed on the great day of the feast, "Let anyone who is thirsty come to me, and let the one who believes in me drink. As the scripture has said, 'Out of the believer's heart shall flow rivers of living water'" (John 7:37-38). The resources of God are inexhaustible. The Holy Spirit is offered to all people, and he is able to satisfy each and every believer.

When we come to God and tell him we need the Spirit, he will never be annoyed, wondering why we are back. He screams out, inviting us to come to him whenever we thirst. And when we come to ask for more of the Spirit, he will gladly give to us. The Father does not think twice, for he knows how much we need the Holy Spirit. We need his ministry to help us be witnesses. Dallas Willard put it this way in his book *The Divine Conspiracy*: "The function of the Holy Spirit is, first, to move within our souls, and especially our minds, to present the person of Jesus and the reality of his Kingdom. This is through the word of the gospel, in contrast to the realities of life without God."

We must be careful about what we ask for. Do we even want the Holy Spirit if he is going to lead us into becoming witnesses for Jesus? On the surface, of course, we say yes. We are too sophisticated to say no. But deep in our hearts, we must wrestle with the ministry of the Holy Spirit. If we are not experiencing the Spirit empowering us for effective witness, it is not on God; it is on us. God gives without measure.

SPIRITUAL ORGANIZATIONAL CHARTS

Why then are we all not more passionate and effective witnesses? I think we need to be reintroduced to the ministry of the Holy Spirit. Like an organization that has all the right people in all the wrong spots, we have the Holy Spirit in a role that does not maximize his supreme spiritual ministry. Jim Collins commented on this concept in *Good to Great*, his study on great and enduring companies and how they achieved and maintained incredible success.

They [the executives who ignited the transformations from good to great companies] said in essence, "Look, I don't really know where we should take this bus. But I know this much: If we get the right people on the bus, the right people in the right seats, and the wrong people off the bus, then we'll figure out how to take it someplace great."

The Holy Spirit has been in the wrong seat on the bus far too long. His talents include being the absolute best in the world at empowering witnesses to speak about Jesus. That is his joy and passion. He would do that in his sleep (if he ever slept). He is internationally famous for directing powerful evangelism movements of God, performing deeds of power and bringing multitudes of sinners to profound conviction of their own lostness and desperate need for God.

Yet we often confine him to the role of encouraging people with his presence during our worship. We might invite him to our prayer meetings, even ask for his healing powers to be released. And certainly Christians are lined up around the block for his counseling ministry to break into our personal struggles. But according to John 3:34 and John 16:7, his résumé is all about witness. The Holy Spirit is in the wrong seat on the bus of our Christian ministries. He is the five-star general of all spiritual warfare and advancement, yet we have him licking envelopes in the mailroom. The Spirit is gracious, and while we in no way control him, we can impede his work.

The résumé, talents and ministry of the Spirit must become concretely expressed in our lives. That is what it means to glorify God. When the Spirit moves, we will experience his work as the missionary David Brainerd did, as he saw the Holy Spirit work in the heart of a native woman who had for six years been hard to the ministry of God's Word in her life. Consider this testimony from Brainerd's journals:

> This woman appeared to have the most humbling sense of her own meanness and unworthiness, her weakness and inability to

preserve herself from sin, and to persevere in the way of holiness, crying, "If I live, I shall sin." I then thought I had never seen such an appearance of ecstasy and humility meeting in any one person in all my life before. (*The Life and Diary of David Brainerd*, ed. Jonathan Edwards)

Why should the Spirit be sorting catalogs in the mailroom when he can convict people and make them alive in Jesus? What do our eyes see the Spirit doing in our witness ministries? Do we see what Brainerd saw? Is the Spirit alive in our evangelism?

LIVE IN THE SPIRIT

The reasons we say no to God and his measureless Spirit are multiple and complex. I would like to focus on one. I believe that we say no to the Spirit because we do not know that it is really the Spirit speaking to us. It is as if a friend is calling on the phone but we don't recognize the voice. So we carry on with the conversation, hoping it will soon become clear who we are speaking with. With God's Spirit, however, we sometimes engage in conversation, thinking it is someone else. We hear from him regularly, but we think it is ourselves. Here is how this works.

When was the last time you had a thought to share Jesus' gospel with someone? Was it someone at the office, a family member, a close friend going through a difficult time, a stranger in line at the market? If you are like me, you hear those thoughts in your mental world all the time. Often I discount that as my own idea and quickly come up with five reasons why it is not the "perfect time" to introduce someone to Jesus. (As if a perfect time ever existed.)

Yet when I read the New Testament, I see the theme of human sinfulness dominating the pages. If we, as Paul taught, are wretched beings who have no good inside us (Romans 7:20-24), where does this call to witness come from? Paul urged us to believe that there is no good inside of us apart from what God has graciously implanted in our being. Might it be that the idea of sharing our faith (which is arguably the greatest single act of love one human being can do for another) is the good that God graciously puts into our wretched beings?

I do not believe that every thought about sharing Jesus comes directly from the Holy Spirit. I am sure that many of us have had excellent training to shape our worldview and trigger our responses to open our heart and mouth. However, I would bet my last dollar that we all regularly ignore words of direction from the Holy Spirit. We believe that the call somehow originates inside us, and therefore we find reasons to discount the leading. In doing so, we quench the Spirit who has been given to us without measure. And we ignore direct leadership from God, the One who sends us to people he is at work in.

CHOOSING GROWTH

After studying John 3:34, I made a covenant with God that has changed my personal evangelism ministry. If the Holy Spirit is given without measure to help me speak the words of God, I want to embrace every opportunity I am led into. So I told God that when those ideas, inklings and leadings pop into my mind, I will assume it is God and act with faith to see if it is. I figured that if the leading is from God, I will surely know. I also figured that if it isn't from God, I will likely find out even more quickly. I have taken more than a few ego blows because of this commitment to God, but I am a much stronger witness for it.

I invite you to make a similar commitment with God. Would you consider assuming that the inklings and hunches to witness that pop into your heart and mind are from God? Assume it is a memo from the company's greatest employee, who is locked in the mailroom. He wants to get the word out! You will certainly be stretched and challenged, but I also know you will experience some of the measureless power of the Spirit of God. Here are four ways I have seen the Spirit of God execute his ministry of empowering effective witness.

Direction. The Spirit of God loves to give the witness direction. He is the general in the war against evil and loves to be in constant communication with the soldiers in the field. He sees what we on the frontlines cannot see. Therefore, one of his most strategic ministries is to direct the ones he sends to where the Father is at work. As one of my mentors has taught me, God can do more in one moment than we can do in ten years. We must train our ears to hear the voice of the Spirit and train our feet to go where he directs.

In the fall of 2000 I challenged students in a year-long evangelism program to assume that the inklings and leadings were from God and to go with the Spirit. I told them they would be embarrassed *and* they would experience the evangelism ministry of the Spirit. As a community of young and scared witnesses, we prayed for more of the Holy Spirit and committed to speaking God's words. God was faithful to give us more of the Spirit.

Steve, a junior from UCLA, was praying at the student union. He was enjoying his quiet time and told the Spirit that he wanted to be used for witness. He created space for God by settling his heart, sitting quietly and listening for the Spirit to speak to him. As he strained to listen, he heard a small inner voice say to him, "Woman in the pink shirt." He sure didn't expect God to say that. Was that from the Spirit? He lifted his head from prayer and looked around him, scanning the patio until he saw the person sitting right behind him. He almost hyperventilated when he saw a woman in a pink shirt. What should he do now? Steve certainly didn't feel prepared to talk with her.

Assuming the word was from God, Steve asked God for some good old-fashioned courage, took a deep breath and walked to her table. He opened his mouth and out flowed streams of babble and gibberish. To this day he swears he might as well have been speaking a foreign language. Somehow the woman picked up the pieces of the dangling conversation. "What are you studying?" she asked.

"I am reading the Bible," Steve replied.

"Wow, what a coincidence! I was just telling my friend the other day that I was really interested in reading the Bible. But I am having trouble understanding it."

"I have been studying the Bible for three years. It has changed my life."

"Do you think you could help me understand the Bible? Maybe we could get together and you could be a sort of Bible mentor."

Steve and the woman agreed on a time and place for their first GIG. When testifying about his deed of faith, Steve beamed at his intimate experience with God. He listened to the Holy Spirit, and the Spirit directed him to someone the Father was drawing. The woman even invited herself to his GIG.

The Father gives the Spirit without measure so that he will direct us to those who are being drawn into faith.

Prayerful intercession. The Spirit of God will put people on our heart to pray for. We are called to pray for our non-Christian friends, but there are certain people whom God's Spirit will put deeper into our hearts. The Spirit will somehow communicate with our spirit, interfacing to let us know our consistent prayer will be a part of their conversion. For those whom God calls us particularly to stand in the gap, the Spirit will lead us into intimate, powerful and persevering prayer for their salvation.

During my first year at UCLA, God sovereignly chose Karen Ji to be my neighbor. I am forever grateful. I was not a Christian and was a magnet for dorm controversy. I was written up five times for community violations, including numerous alcohol violations and throwing my roommate's mattress out our eighth-story window. My friends and I would often return from the bar scene at 2:00 a.m. to play full-contact basketball in my dorm room. Karen slept on the other side of the paper-thin dorm wall. Karen had 8:00 a.m. classes that entire first semester.

Karen was a deep believer and turned to the Holy Spirit for leadership as I became a growing problem in her life. The Holy Spirit spoke to Karen and gave her kingdom eyes to see me with. She saw me as someone who was lost, inconsiderate and searching for something to heal the pain in life. She didn't see a loser neighbor; she saw someone who was desperate for Jesus. I just didn't know it. During the first week of school, Karen committed to praying for me every single day. Later that year I became a follower of Jesus. She had prayed me into the kingdom! I converted in May and our academic year ended in June. As we moved out of the dorm, we said we would stay in touch. But I didn't see her the next three years at UCLA. I bet she wondered more than once if I continued on the path of discipleship.

Four years later I saw Karen at Urbana, InterVarsity's missions conference in Urbana, Illinois. The evening plenary session had just released and I was among the twenty thousand students who flooded out into the cold, snowy night to head for the buses. As I stood in line, I heard someone say, "John?" It was Karen. She was at Urbana leading her church's college group into world missions. She was shocked to see me. The last time I saw her, I had been a Christian for roughly thirty days. I told her that I was now a campus minister with InterVarsity. Knowing where I had come from and what I had been through, she was so happy that she began to cry. I hugged her and thanked her for listening to God's Spirit and praying me into the kingdom.

The Father gives the Spirit without measure so that we will pray for the spiritual rebirth of our friends.

Word of knowledge. The Spirit of God will give us words of knowledge to help convince non-Christians to put their faith in God. Jesus himself modeled a word of knowledge in evangelism multiple times as recorded in John's Gospel. He used a word of knowledge to call Simon Peter and Nathanael. He spoke otherwise unknowable in-

formation to the woman at the well, referring to her five former husbands and the man she was currently with. This word of knowledge
led to the salvation of the entire Samaritan village. I've seen similar
uses of the word of knowledge in witness.

Linda was not a follower of Jesus and had some blocks that made
it difficult for her to commit to Christ. She had seen Jesus in Mark's
Gospel but told me that she just couldn't commit to following him.
Her father was a recent convert to African American Islam, and she
didn't want to disrupt the family by committing to Christ. As she studied the Word, she knew that Jesus was wonderful, and she had a great
"sense" he would change her life for the better. She testified that she
understood the gospel and wanted to respond but that her father
wouldn't understand.

On the last night of our conference, the Holy Spirit ministered to
the students through the Word and intimately touched our hearts as
we worshiped. While many of the other students responded with
fresh commitments and tears of joy, Linda was unmoved. I asked
God to give me a special word for Linda so that she would know that
God knew her personally and would take care of her. I listened for
the Holy Spirit to speak a word of knowledge to me. As I listened, I
heard the name Richelle.

While the music continued, I pulled Linda to the side and told
her that I speak to God and that sometimes he will speak to me. We
were in the middle of an urgent ministry moment, and I couldn't
whip up a better explanation on the spot, so I was relieved when she
said that sounded normal enough for her. I told her I prayed that God
would tell me something that would prove he knew her personally
and would take care of her. She got more excited. I asked her, "Does
the name Richelle mean anything to you?"

At first she didn't answer. It seemed like an hour passed before she
spoke again. She finally nodded her head without making eye contact. She was feeling shame.

"Why would God tell me to tell you that?"

"Richelle is the name of the new girl my ex-boyfriend left me for."

Immediately fireworks went off in my soul! Linda had been carrying the profound pain of being dumped for another. I gave her a hug as she began to cry. I told her that Jesus was absolutely nothing like her ex-boyfriend. He is the Great Bridegroom and is faithful and loving. I promised her that Jesus will never abandon her or make her feel unwanted in the least. She seemed to take in my exhortation.

I then told her that God does not give words of knowledge to just anybody and that she needed to respond to Jesus with the same intensity that he was initiating with to break into her life. She thought about the offer to follow Jesus and said she would pray about it that night.

Sadly, to this day (as far as I know), Linda has not committed to following Jesus. Even with a word of knowledge from God, she chose to live her life alone and try to take care of herself. Yet from Linda's example, may we be encouraged to seek the Spirit of God for fresh power in our witness.

The Father gives the Spirit without measure so that we can engage the world with knowledge we otherwise would not know.

Miracles and healing. The Spirit of God will perform miraculous acts of power through us to authenticate the gospel message to help the non-Christian follow Jesus. The unbelieving world has never been more open to receiving the power of God into their lives. One real experience with the Holy Spirit can shape an entire worldview. Our friends are eager to experience God in their lives. We must pray for them. God will get involved.

Will was furious. He had just gotten into a verbal altercation outside the student lounge at Compton Community College. He wanted to fight the man who was badgering him, but he didn't want to go to jail. So he stuffed his anger and went inside the student lounge to try and burn off his anger.

Will had been a friend of the InterVarsity ministry at Compton for a couple of months. I talked sports with him, but he was never interested enough to come to our preaching service or join a GIG. As I approached him that day, I could tell something was wrong. I asked him what had happened to make him so mad. I told him he did the right thing in not fighting and put my arm around him. I then asked him if I could pray for him.

As I prayed for Will, I immediately felt God's presence fall on us right in the Compton College student lounge. There were students sitting at the tables next to us, carrying on with their business, not noticing that Will and I were having a serious Spirit moment. I sheepishly looked around, wondering what people might think about this very private, but also public, spiritual moment we were experiencing.

As we prayed, with God's Spirit very present with us, the word that came to my mouth was *peace*. I must have said it ten times in a row. My hand felt hot as I laid it on Will's shoulder. I kept ushering in God's peace. I looked at Will. He had burst into tears right in the student lounge. His spirit had been touched and he was enjoying the peace of God.

When we stopped praying, I asked him what had happened to him. He told me that he felt deep waves of peace and that God took away his anger. He then confessed to me, "John, I have heard about God and his love many times. I even went to church for a while. But that is the first time I have ever experienced him."

Right after that, we left the student lounge. I found my ministry partner Mailin Chu, and together we shared the gospel with Will. That day, after experiencing his power, Will became a follower of Jesus. He went on to become one of our first IVCF student leaders at Compton.

The Father gives the Spirit without measure so that we can experience his power to authenticate the message of the gospel.

HOW MUCH CAN YOU HANDLE?

The Holy Spirit is given to us that we might speak the words of God. The Spirit has the best witness résumé in the universe. He wants to perform his ministry through the sent ones of God.

God knows that you and I are the least likely candidates to be sent for witness. That is why he gives the Spirit without measure. As we state our need, God will immediately provide not cups of the Holy Spirit but oceans upon oceans, that we might drink of his love and have that love roar out of our hearts like a river. What do you need in your witness? God gives the Spirit without measure.

How much can you handle?

KEY CONCEPTS

The Father's gift of the Holy Spirit

• The Holy Spirit is given generously by the Father.

• He gives the Spirit to his children without measure.

• If we don't experience the Spirit in our lives, it is on us, not God.

The ministry of the Spirit

• The ones who are sent speak God's word because of the Spirit.

• The Holy Spirit has the unique job of convicting the world of sin.

• The Spirit is invited into roles that display his greatness in witness.

The witness empowered by God

• God will give us the Spirit for direction in our witness.

• God will give us the Spirit for intercession for our witness.

• God will give us the Spirit for hidden knowledge in our witness.

• God will give us the Spirit for power in our witness.

GROWTH STEP

Reflect on how much of the Holy Spirit you experience in your witness.

1. Will you make a covenant with God to assume the Spirit is speaking to you to lead you to non-Christians?

2. In what areas of your evangelism do you most desire the Holy Spirit to take leadership?

3. What practical steps can you take to experience his greatness in evangelism?

SEVEN

FOLLOWED BY JESUS

It is no longer because of what you said that we believe,
for we have heard for ourselves,
and we know that this is truly the Savior of the world.

THE PEOPLE OF SYCHAR

I love watching the summer Olympics. It is such a treat to see the world's best athletes come together to compete for gold. I particularly enjoy the opening ceremony. Admittedly the stadium productions are getting a bit over the top, but I always seem to shed a tear on opening night. When a lone representative from a small country marches into the stadium, proudly carrying his or her national flag, my tears start flowing. I think of the long, hard road of training it took to reach the Olympics. I imagine how thrilled an athlete's family must be as they suddenly see someone they love in one of the world's grandest events. I always experience this as a small appetizer of what the apostle John saw in his great vision of God's city, where every tongue and tribe will worship Jesus (Revelation 7:9-10).

At the 2000 Olympic Games in Sydney, Australia, Marion Jones was the story. She became the first woman to win five medals at the same Olympics. She won three gold and two bronze medals. She ran the anchor leg for the U.S. women in the 400-meter relay. She then turned around and three hours later ran an amazing third leg in the 1,600-meter relay to win the American team the gold. Here is the Associated Press's account of the 1,600-meter relay:

> Jones ran a spectacular 1600 meter relay. Jones was a stride be-
> hind Deon Hemmings of Jamaica when she got the baton, but
> had a 15-meter lead when she handed off to Latasha Colander-
> Richardson—who struggled at the end, but held on for the victory.
>
> Jones' split time was 49.4 seconds. Monique Hennagan, who
> ran the second leg and handed the baton to Jones, faded at the
> end and had dropped to second place.
>
> "I was just hoping she didn't take off too fast, because I didn't
> have anything left," Hennagan said. "Then I gave it to her and
> I saw her open up. Thank God she lit the burners."

Competing and winning as a team is what Olympic relays are all
about. Hennagan and Jones together won the gold that night in Sydney. Jones was definitely the star, but they won it together.

In that same spirit of team, more than we might think, Jesus invites us to win the world with him through witness. He is certainly
the brightest, boldest and most brilliant star in all the universe. He is
the Son of God, the perfect One, reflecting the incomparable glory
of God. He alone will be honored and worshiped for all the ages to
come. Yet Jesus lowers himself to align himself with us. He was bap-
tized even though he did not have to be. He calls himself our brother
(John 20:17). While being the lofty and holy One who makes demons
scream at his presence, he invites us onto his evangelism team. And
when Jesus lights the burners, we cannot lose.

BODY LANGUAGE SPEAKS VOLUMES

Body language is important. You can often learn more truth from
body language than you can from the spoken word. Description of
body language can paint wonderful pictures. In Revelation 4, for example, God is described as sitting on his throne. He never lifts a fin-
ger; he only speaks. In fact, throughout the whole book, God never

gets up from his throne. He sits, in full authority, as the reigning Supreme Person, who is in charge of every single detail in all the universe. The only movement that comes from the throne is God's word moving forth, as all of his decrees become instant reality.

As you go out into the world to deliver witness, can you picture Jesus watching your ministry? Though it might sound a bit unorthodox, I believe we all carry mental pictures of Jesus. Henri Nouwen writes in *Compassion*, "How do we know that God is our God and not a stranger, an outsider, a passerby? We know this because in Jesus, God's compassion became visible to us." If you were to snap a photograph of Jesus while he watched you minister as a witness, what would God's Son be saying with his body language? Whatever it is, it says a lot about your understanding of God and evangelism.

Would Jesus' arms be crossed because he is impatient? Would he be looking off in another direction because he doesn't take your witness seriously? Might he be wincing a bit because the GIG you are leading is going so poorly? Might he be tapping his foot, wondering when you are going to get it together?

Or do you think Jesus might be excited that you are sharing your faith? Could it be that he is getting the attention of others, calling them to observe your faith, because he is so proud of you? Could he be nodding in approval after you handle a particularly challenging apologetic question?

Or could he be observing with even greater interest, for personal reasons? What if he is waiting, like Marion Jones, for you to hand him the baton, so that he can himself participate in the race to win that person? What if you weren't only Jesus' child, or his object of grace, but his teammate in the great cause of evangelism in the world?

I have a feeling that if we saw Jesus' body language as we gave our witness, we would be ashamed at how hard we are on ourselves. He is full of grace and truth. And he participates in our witness.

TROUBLED BY THE TEXT

In the fall of 1998 I committed to a personal growth project of studying all of John's Gospel. I set out to master John. After my study reached the end, however, I realized that I had been mastered by John.

In the midst of digging deeper into John's Gospel and his razor-sharp theology, I came across an interesting passage that I had previously overlooked: "[Jesus] went away again across the Jordan to the place where John had been baptizing earlier, and he remained there. Many came to him, and they were saying, 'John performed no sign, but everything that John said about this man was true.' And many believed in him there" (John 10:40-42). This snippet is one of many transition paragraphs that serve as bridges to the next section. They normally appear when Jesus is physically on the move to a new city. But this section is different. It contains more detailed information than the previous connector paragraphs. It reintroduces us to John the Baptist's ministry, though our last update came some seven chapters earlier. I was caught and I began to look closer.

I suddenly saw themes and language similar to John's account of the Samaritan village coming to faith. I felt like a prospector who had just hit gold with his pick! This was no filler paragraph; I had stumbled upon some of Jesus' own philosophy of witness. I quickly began to compare and contrast more thoroughly this account with that of the woman at the well. As I did so, Jesus' theory of witness became clearer and clearer. Where I had already seen the Father's role and the ministry of the Holy Spirit, for the first time I saw Jesus' own role in bringing people to faith.

John repeated a theme seven times in the Fourth Gospel: Jesus follows his witnesses. That number is significant. The number seven is the number of God's completion, his wholeness and his victory. And Jesus followed witnesses seven times. Whenever a witness would go before Jesus, preparing the way by declaring the words of life to a group of people, Jesus would then physically follow that witness to personally visit the people. Seven times he spent time with the people personally, and the spiritual impact was invariably the same: the result of Jesus' follow-up was genuine faith and the conversion of the hearers, and deepening of the witnesses' faith.

It was as though Jesus' traveling and ministry schedule was determined by the ministry of his witnesses. If a witness gave testimony in Capernaum, Jesus would go to Capernaum. If John was evangelizing by the river, Jesus made sure he went to follow up the word there. As his witnesses got the word out, the Word would follow the word. The Son of God performed the follow-up himself! That is what it means that Jesus is the great sprinter who runs the final leg in our witness relays. Just as Hennagan prepared the way for Jones, so our words of witness prepare the way for Jesus' words of life.

Interestingly, this pattern did not always mean success. Sometimes, when his witnesses physically traveled to a place to preach the good news, the word was rejected there. But even in those instances Jesus still did follow-up; he just reached out to a different group of people. He would find his witnesses who had been rejected. He would lift their spirits. He would heal their wounds and lead them into deep worship. He would also back them up by giving a word of challenge to those who had rejected the truth of his witnesses.

The chart below identifies the seven witnesses, highlights their ministry of witness and records how Jesus followed as the word went out.

Arguably there is an eighth witness that Jesus follows. The apostle John and his book serve as the eighth witness. John wrote, "Jesus did many other signs in the presence of his disciples, which are not written in this book. But these are written so that you may come to believe that Jesus is the Messiah, the Son of God, and that through believing you may have life in his name" (20:30-31). The Fourth Gospel is the apostle's own witness. He definitely got the word out. In reflecting on the last two thousand years and the powerful impact the

SEVEN WITNESSES

1. John the Baptist

John Gives Witness—John 1:19-36
At Bethany across the Jordan, the whole country hears from John that someone is coming who will baptize them with the Holy Spirit. John experiences persecution from the religious leaders for his witness. We are given no immediate report of the fruit from his witness.

Jesus Follows John's Witness—John 10:40-42
After three years, Jesus arrives at the community beyond the Jordan where John gave witness. He stays with them and validates John's witness. The result is that many believe in him there.

2. Andrew

Andrew Gives Witness—John 1:40-41
Andrew is one of the first two disciples to follow Jesus. He spends a day with Jesus, and then in his excitement and zeal over what he has found, he gives witness to his brother, Simon Peter.

Jesus Follows Andrew's Witness—John 1:42
Jesus meets Peter and immediately gives him a prophetic word of what God will make him into. Simon becomes one of Jesus' three inner-circle leaders.

3. Philip

Philip Gives Witness—John 1:43-45
Philip is told personally by Jesus to follow him. His first act of faith is going to Nathanael and giving him witness that they have found the One whom Moses and the prophets wrote about in Holy Scripture.

Jesus Follows Philip's Witness—John 1:47-51
Jesus meets Nathanael with a prophetic word revealing the innermost passions and dreams of Nathanael. The previously resistant, jaded and racist zealot becomes putty in Jesus' hands and follows him.

4. The Woman at the Well

The Woman Gives Witness—John 4:28-30
The woman at the well is given living water and commits to Jesus. She is immediately transformed, drops her water jar and crosses every known barrier to announce to her community that she thinks she has found the Christ.

SEVEN WITNESSES (cont.)

Jesus Follows the Woman's Witness—John 4:30-42
The villagers come to Jesus because of the woman's witness. Their partial belief is solidified after spending two days with Jesus. The result is that many more come to believe in Jesus because they have heard for themselves and know that Jesus is the Savior of the world.

5. The Blind Man

The Blind Man Gives Witness—John 9:8-34
The man born blind is healed by Jesus. Ironically, those around him cannot see that Jesus healed him. He endures multiple rounds of interrogation and persecution on account of his healing. Because of his witness, he is cast out of society.

Jesus Follows the Blind Man's Witness—John 9:35-38
After remaining in the background during the unfolding developments, Jesus leaps into action when the man is cast out. Jesus finds the man to tell him he is the Son of Man. The blind man is the first person to see that Jesus is the living God come to earth. He worships him, and Jesus receives his worship.

6. Mary Magdalene

Mary Gives Witness—John 20:18
Mary is the first person to interact with Jesus in resurrection form. She is commanded to give witness to the other disciples that he is alive. There is no full report of the actual words she uses in her witness.

Jesus Follows Mary's Witness—John 20:19-23
Jesus affirms Mary's testimony with his presence. The result is that Jesus sends his disciples out for witness and empowers them with the Holy Spirit in their apostolic ministry that changes the world forever.

7. The Ten Disciples

The Disciples Give Witness—John 20:24-25
For some reason, Thomas missed the first visit from the resurrected Lord. When he finally shows up, the other disciples tell Thomas, "We have seen the Lord."

Jesus Follows the Disciples' Witness—John 20:26-29
Jesus fulfills every requirement that Thomas needs for true belief. Thomas responds to the wounds of Christ with powerful testimony of Jesus' deity and pledges his allegiance to Jesus.

book of John has had upon the world, we have to admit that Jesus has powerfully followed the witness of the apostle John.

WITNESS LESSON 1—
JESUS CAN CLOSE THE DEAL

Knowing that Jesus follows his witnesses should change the way we approach evangelism. First, it should take the pressure off. We do not need to be perfect. Jesus is the master of follow-up. Whoever we give our witness to, whatever their circumstances and whatever their unique blocks, Jesus can handle it. He brought faith to Samaritan villages, Jewish peasants, members of the Sanhedrin, fishermen and blind people. He has seen it all and can perform that which we cannot.

Our witness, inadequate as it may seem to us, will be good enough for Jesus to work with. He follows the words of witnesses as articulate and powerful as John the Baptist and as unrefined and choppy as the man born blind. Jesus dominates the closing process of evangelism. It is our role to get the witness out and into the lives of the people. It is our role to draw out their curiosity about Jesus and teach them the gospel as faithful witnesses. But again, God does not want us to live under the pressure of thinking that it is all about us and our ability to change hearts. Jesus specializes in giving people new hearts. He is definitely the most valuable player on our evangelism team! We must pass the baton and see him win the souls of lost sinners.

WITNESS LESSON 2—
THE MORE WITNESS, THE BETTER

If we are witnesses who prepare the way for Jesus and his own effective evangelism ministry, and if he does indeed follow our witness to give life to others, we should be drenching the whole world in witness. We should be confident, eager and passionate witnesses because we know that the One who follows our witness can do all things well. Our witness should go far and wide, touching as many people as possible.

The fact that Jesus is the greatest of all does not mean we can be passive in our own development. We should long to become better teammates of Jesus—sent ones who are more skilled, bolder and more comfortable with giving witness to everyone we know. When witness is delivered, Jesus takes it upon himself to do the follow-up. What could be more liberating and joy-filled than knowing that Jesus himself will somehow and someway follow up our witness? The better our witness, the more Jesus has to work with.

WITNESS LESSON 3—
THE GOOD TEAMMATE

As we run our leg of the great witness race, we must picture Jesus as following us. I believe that we focus too much on ourselves and not enough on his greatness to change the hearts of sinners into true worshipers. If we are honest, I think we all believe on some level that God is frustrated with us as teammates. Deep in our hearts, we might envision Jesus on the track with his hands folded, wondering what is taking us so long and when we will get it together.

It is common for superstars to be hard on their teammates. While desiring to make their teammates better, a superstar can often treat them poorly and disrespect them, causing them to believe that the superstar is merely putting up with them. This intensity and critical spirit, highlighted by Sam Smith's *The Jordon Rules*, marked Michael Jordan's career and legacy as the ultimate NBA superstar. Do we picture Jesus of Nazareth, star player on the evangelism team, as similarly impatient with us?

On our darkest of days, we might think Jesus is talking to the other teammates about what losers we are. Of course, we might be too sophisticated to admit this publicly, but we may quietly believe that Jesus wants other people, like Peter, Paul or the woman at the well, to be on his team. He surely accepts Billy Graham's work as one who is sent. But our great fear is that he looks at our witness and scratches his head, wondering why he puts up with us on his team. If that is our picture of Jesus, we will surely fake an injury, come up lame and never get back on the track. But that's not reality. Jesus is the good doctor, full of compassion, who loves his teammates.

Being a witness involves great amounts of suffering and rejection. So it is easy to understand why we are so emotionally sensitive in this area. But it is the fight of faith to believe the promises of God and the love of God even in our evangelism. As we relate with God over witness, we find it hard to give God the benefit of the doubt that he might actually like us. We are quick to articulate the reasons why God would be disappointed in us. And in evangelism, we will always be able to find ten blemishes at any given moment. God is far more committed to us as witnesses, and he is far more encouraging than we give him credit for.

I am not basing this belief on some self-help book I read or on an interview I saw on a talk show. God's support and his love for his witnesses can be seen in his actions. No matter who Jesus' witnesses were, he backed them up! If you are a witness, he will follow you. You are not alone.

WHEN DOES JESUS BACK UP WITNESS?

In studying John's teaching of Jesus following his witnesses, two questions arise. When does God back up his witnesses? And what about those who reject the witness?

We see from John's Gospel that Jesus follows up the word that has gotten out, both immediately and over long periods of time. It is his choice. And in John's theology, knowing that the Son only does what he sees the Father doing, we can conclude that God the Father sends Jesus at different times according to his sovereign wisdom.

God is gentle as he births people into the kingdom. He takes into account those he is drawing and how much they can handle. He doesn't want to speed the process up so greatly that the delicate will not be able to respond in their love relationship to Christ. He also takes into account the unique issues of loyalty, success or failure that each witness grapples with. It might not be a season of harvesting, yet Jesus following witness is meant to be good for everyone, both convert and disciple. Whether Jesus follows the witness immediately or over the course of a longer time period, his timing is impeccable.

Jesus follows his witnesses—four weeks. Connie Huang is a Christian today because she met Jesus in a GIG. She did not come from a Christian home and she did not go to college to look for God. But God was looking for her.

Through friendships with people who took their faith seriously, Connie was ready to take her first steps to investigate Jesus for herself. She came to a worship service and immediately noticed the passion and the fervor that her friends had for God. She then heard a sermon from Luke 15 and rapidly identified herself as the lost sheep that the Good Shepherd was searching for. After the sermon, she met with others who wanted to take the next step. She decided to join a GIG and began studying Jesus' biographies.

Connie came to her first GIG and brought her friend Laura, who was also a non-Christian. For the next four weeks, the word got out and got deep into their hearts. Connie's soul was being touched by the Word and she could tell that things were changing. The changes weren't dramatic to the untrained eye. She wasn't smoking crack or stealing cars. But she did begin to experience Jesus opening her eyes to her own selfish nature. It soon became clear to her how little she knew and trusted God for her future.

At the end of our third GIG, it was clear that Jesus' word was moving powerfully in Connie's life. The day before she left for spring break, she was challenged to consider following Jesus. She said she was open to it and would pray about it.

That week Jesus followed up the witness. Every day of her break, Connie felt a steady and sure conviction about her need for God.

She was overwhelmed with the darkness inside of her and cried out to Jesus for rescue.

Connie began following Jesus later that year. Her friend Laura, whom she had first brought to the GIG because she felt uncomfortable, followed close behind. Connie proved instrumental in Laura's conversion. Today both are active servants in their local church in Los Angeles.

The word was given. Jesus followed the witness over the course of one month. Connie came to belief not because of what the GIG said but because of what Jesus said to her.

Jesus follows his witnesses—three years. For years, my good friend Jeff Hanson has led GIGs in his real estate office. He has learned much about persistence and waiting on the Lord's timing from his relationship with Joanne. She was trapped in a cult for three years. But Jeff continually prayed and shared with Joanne about God's great work in his own life. His words never made an immediate impact on her. In fact, she often responded to his witness with witness of her own, trying to recruit him into her cult.

At the end of the third year, things began to get tougher for Joanne. The cult leader was putting pressure on her to move into deeper levels of leadership. She confided to Jeff that for years she had seen his life—his freedom in God, his ability to love people and his peace—and she knew that what he had was the real deal. She told him that she wanted to get out of her cult and follow the God he knew. Jeff began leading her into the process of leaving the cult. She confided to him that her biggest fear was dealing with her regional leader, a woman named Connie (definitely a different Connie from the previous story).

Joanne met with Connie to tell her she was leaving the cult. It did not go well. Connie manipulated her with the guilt trip that she was the only hope of her parents finding God. She declared that God now hated Joanne and that he would never speak to her again. Joanne was torn to pieces by Connie.

Jeff brought Joanne over to my house and we prayed for Joanne. We asked God to protect her from Connie's lies and to break through to help her know what was true and that he still loved her.

The next day Joanne had her final meeting with Connie. She was terrified and at this point did not know which end was up. She wavered and thought about staying in the cult. As the clock hit 5:00 p.m., Jeff began praying that God would empower Joanne for her meeting with Connie that evening.

Joanne left her downtown L.A. building and walked through some of the homeless folks toward the parking garage. One of the homeless people was a woman, around forty years old, barefoot and with her hair disheveled. The odd thing about this woman was that she had on a stunning floral dress. The bright colors caught Joanne's attention, so she looked in the woman's direction and the two made eye contact. The woman gestured her near. Joanne stopped to listen.

The woman said to Joanne, "Connie is of the devil! Connie is of the devil!" She then walked casually down the street as if nothing had happened. The messenger had delivered the message she had been sent for.

The woman said only two sentences, but those two sentences changed Joanne's life. God was real. He didn't hate her and he had spoken powerfully to free her from the clutches of the cult. It took over three years, but Jesus followed Jeff's witness to win Joanne.

Jesus follows his witnesses—rejection. It is strong medicine for weak souls that Jesus follows his witnesses. It is wonderful when we are able to see clearly God's great work in the conversion of sinners. But what do we do when we give witness and the person is hard toward the gospel? What does Jesus do when people reject the words of life?

Allan was a friend of mine who was nominally interested in his parents' religion. He would talk about his devotion often, but I wondered what exactly it was that he was devoted to. He was a secular humanist who liked a religion that fit in with his American dream and the sensual pleasures he sought. We spent an evening together, and our conversation casually began to turn toward the things of God.

He asked me why I thought Jesus was real. I gave him all the empirical evidence I knew. It didn't convince him in the least. He came up with his own evidence for why my theories were invalid.

I then chose another approach and told him of my personal experiences with God. I tried my best to paint myself as a needy sinner who is filled by the love of God. I even shared how I had experienced Jesus in my personal prayer that very morning. I thought I really had him on that one. There was no way he could discount my personal experience of Jesus.

Allan almost fell out of his chair laughing. He had to ask me to repeat myself because he couldn't believe what was coming out of my mouth. "You experienced God? He came to you this morning while you were praying? Yeah, right!" I was crushed and felt humiliated. But he kept going on and on. He really enjoyed debating other people and was doing a great job of entertaining himself. For some reason, this hurt more than other rejections I had experienced. I got angry at Allan, said some things that to this day I regret saying and left the conversation trying to regain some of my dignity.

When I returned home, I knelt down and quieted my spirit in front of God. I felt like the blind man who was misunderstood, rejected and thrown out of society. I gave Jesus my fears that Allan would use the information I had told him against me with other friends. I gave God my anger. I gave him my confusion. I thought that everyone was supposed to convert when I shared Jesus with them. I felt defeated and sat with God.

I had fallen on the track as I ran for Jesus. The baton went flying into the crowd. My knee was gushing blood. But Jesus ran to me, his witness, and took care of me. That night Jesus found me and he invited me to worship him. As I sat in his presence, I delighted in how real and how true my God is. Others may laugh, but he is the ever-flowing river of living water that my soul needs to drink. Jesus followed my feeble attempts at witness in order to pick me up and bless me.

From that night my relationship with Allan was chilly. He thought I was a village idiot. But I didn't sweat that any longer. Jesus of Nazareth had my back.

BACKED BY GOD

God does not send us alone into the world to give witness. If you are into Lone Ranger evangelism, you should find a different religion to promote. God the Father is always at work. He sends us where he has already been and stands behind us. God the Holy Spirit is inside of us, empowering us to speak the words of God. And God the Son is in back of us, eager to finish the work of evangelism and transform the heart of the sinner.

The process of evangelism, from beginning to end, is dominated by God. Our role in winning the world is actually rather small. But our role *is* critical. Will we live sent, filled and followed? Will we get the word out?

KEY CONCEPTS

Jesus following his witnesses

- John's Gospel highlights seven witnesses.
- Jesus followed all of the witnesses as they got the word out.
- The result was genuine faith, commitment and worship.

The body language of Jesus

- Jesus' body language as we witness reveals our evangelism theology.
- Jesus is more gracious and encouraging than we think.
- He knows that he can make up any deficit in our witness.

Timing and rejection

- Jesus will sometimes follow witness immediately.
- Other times, Jesus will act patiently to bring about the most good.
- Jesus follows his rejected witnesses, offering himself as encouragement.

GROWTH STEPS

Reflect on how Jesus has followed your witness as you have prepared his way with the Word of God.

1. How does Jesus' following up witnesses empower you? Which person or group must you talk to?
2. In what relationships have you seen Jesus follow your witness?
3. With what time frames have you seen Jesus follow your witness?
4. How has he followed you as you have suffered rejection, pain and discouragement on account of his name?

BLISTERS OR CALLUSES?

How Witnesses Grow

*Whoever is faithful in a very little is faithful also in much;
and whoever is dishonest in a very little is dishonest also in much.*

JESUS OF NAZARETH

Don't just talk about it, be about it!

JUNIOUS LOCKETT

I began to share my faith immediately after I started following Jesus. I shared boldly with anyone who would listen. Sometimes I shared with people who didn't want to listen. I once went up and down an elevator multiple times in a row just so I could tell my story to the elevator man. I loved the captive audience. I am not sure he did, however. I told everyone about the new life I had found in God. I wanted everyone to know that Jesus is real and that he is better than the winning lottery ticket.

But my early witness ministry was not outwardly fruitful. Instead of winning people to Christ, I mostly confused my family and friends. I think I scared more people than I helped. My family had no idea what had gotten into me. They knew I had found something in Jesus, but I did a poor job articulating the new spiritual life I was experiencing. My party friends from high school were amused at my sudden spirituality and were curious about what had happened to me at college. I led them in four GIGs that first summer, but no one responded. I scratched my head and wondered why on earth everyone wasn't following Jesus with me. Did I get the story wrong? Did I leave something out?

I had no idea during that first season that God was more concerned about doing things *in* me than he was about doing things *through* me. He had long-term vision for my growth as an evangelist. I had no idea Jesus was developing me to become a witness who bears fruit not in the moment but over the long haul. I thought I should have arrived as a witness. I had been a Christian for four months, after all.

THE GNAWING PANGS OF GROWTH

For the next five years, as a student leader and campus staff worker with InterVarsity, I grappled with whether or not I was an evangelist. I sensed that calling others to faith was part of my destiny—something God would have me accomplish on earth—mainly because I liked it so much. My friends and colleagues even affirmed that I had the spiritual gift of evangelism. My faith was strengthened and my joy was regularly increased through witness.

But if I was born to be a witness, why wasn't I bearing fruit? Over that five-year period, I saw a handful of people come to Christ through my ministry. But the vast majority of people walked away from me unmoved and unchanged by Jesus' message. Was this the great destiny God had prepared for me?

It would have been easy for me to assume that all the non-Christians who didn't respond to the message were spiritually blind and neck-deep in sin. But God gave me grace to look inward and become a learner with myself as the case study. I began to ask the hard questions of my own witness: *If I am a witness, why am I not more effective? What are my strengths as a witness and how do I capitalize on them? What are my weaknesses as a witness and how do I compensate for them? Why do some people respond to the message and others do not? What is God teaching me about my audience? What must I do to become a more effective evangelist?*

One big lesson I learned was that I lived with an extraordinary amount of pressure upon myself to arrive at a level of success. For some reason I imagined God wanted me way further along than I was. It was like a junior high football player thinking he should be in the NFL. Where did that pressure come from? Not from God. It came from me. But God gave me a long-term growth paradigm. I experienced freedom and perspective to look honestly at the holes in my witness and see where I needed to grow. I began to see my own problems and therefore came up with some ideas of how to allow Jesus to develop me into a witness who bears fruit.

SPIRITUAL GROWTH

Maturing in Christ is sometimes less spiritual than we might imagine. Instead of maturity somehow mysteriously happening to us, it most often comes through our own initiative. Of course, in a theological sense, Jesus is always the source of our growth. But from the human perspective, if we are eager for growth and take steps toward Jesus, we will grow. If we approach growth passively, waiting for a Damascus road experience to launch us into spiritual maturity, we will not grow. Or we will get addicted to life on the mountaintop. Growth does not work that way. The rule of God's kingdom regarding growth is that as you put forth a measure of effort, you will receive back the same measure—and more. But for those who refuse to invest in their own growth, even what they had previously amassed will be taken away (Mark 4:24-25).

Growing as a witness is a choice. Whether you are born for witness and operate powerfully with the spiritual gift of evangelism, or you are just beginning to follow Jesus' call to be sent as a witness, growth awaits you if you give a full effort to become a witness.

What kind of witness will you be in ten years? How about in fifty years? What will be the legacy of love that you will look back on and thank God for? What will be the fruit of your evangelism ministry? The answer tomorrow holds is found in today. The kind of witness you are today will dictate the amount of growth you experience in the future. If you are faithful in a little, you will be faithful in much (Luke 16:10). This is a foundational kingdom rule of growth. If you refuse to give a measure and choose growth today, you should have little confidence that you will be an effective witness in twenty-five years. But if you are faithful today, giving God all of yourself to become a witness, you will likely be a fruitful witness in twenty-five years. How you live today determines what you will become tomorrow.

BLISTERS OR CALLUSES?

Do you have blisters or calluses when it comes to growing as a witness? Blisters happen to people when they try something new. I recently played golf and ended the day with a giant blood blister on the palm of my left hand. Because I hardly ever grab a golf club, and because I had used it all day long, my hand had a severe reaction to the club. My blood blister testified to my lack of experience with golf clubs. But on my right hand I have three major calluses. That is because as a youth I played tennis six days a week, four hours a day, for seven years. The tennis club was my second home. If it wasn't raining, I was usually out hitting balls. My calluses testify to my great passion to become a better tennis player. Blisters form because of experiments; calluses form because of habits.

Jesus would have us all develop witness calluses. As we commit to growing as witnesses, we will be pressed. We will start with blisters and we may want to stop. But we must not stop. We have to allow the habits necessary to become a witness to form. Then we can watch our blisters become calluses. As we form a callus level of commitment to becoming witnesses, Jesus will bless our growth. It won't be easy, but it will be worth it.

Here are a few concepts I have found helpful in my own development as a witness. I have embraced these ideas over and over again and have tried my best to turn them into spiritual habits. May you develop your own calluses that will testify to your personal commitment to being someone who gets the word out.

INTEGRITY CHECKS

God tests his people. I know we don't like that idea. I don't jump for joy when I hear that truth, because I know that I have failed his tests before and will fail future tests. But my not liking the tests does not change their reality. God tested Israel in the wilderness to see what was really in their hearts (Deuteronomy 8:2). Jesus tested Philip by asking him where to find more bread, even though Jesus knew exactly what he was already going to do. He wanted to see what was in Philip's heart (John 6:6). And today Jesus tests us to see what is in our hearts, to see if we will be loyal witnesses.

Living in the reality that God tests us is critical to our continued growth and development. If we know a test is coming, we will likely be prepared. The tests we fail are the ones that surprise us. In high school, when I didn't know a test was coming and the teacher began passing out the papers, butterflies danced wildly in my stomach. I would wish I had known there was going to be a test. I would have studied instead of talking on the phone or watching television. In the same way, we ought to be prepared for the examinations that Jesus gives us to discern our loyalties.

In some ways, we are far worse off than the students squirming in high school classrooms. At least they know when they fail their tests and can learn from their experience to make sure it doesn't happen again. Sadly, we fail integrity checks all the time but don't even know that we were involved in a heart test. When we know that Jesus is giving us opportunities for growth through these checks, we will look for them, be prepared for them and walk with Jesus in faith to deeper levels of witness.

God works through people he can trust. If we consistently communicate to God that we are not open to walking through the doors
of witness that he opens for us, it is only natural that he will give us
our way. The doors will not be opened any longer. Many people
don't experience fruitfulness in their personal witness because they
have proven to God that they are not willing to partner with him and
his evangelism purposes for the world. There are no shortcuts. As we
develop our calluses of witness, we will communicate to God our
willingness and eagerness to bear fruit.

Jesus recently tested my integrity at Borders. I was enjoying God on
my sabbath day, studying John's Gospel. A man approached my table
and began looking over my shoulder. I tried to ignore him. He then
started asking me questions about what I working on. I tried to answer
him quickly. He then began to wax poetic about the Bible. It was my
day off and I wasn't in the mood to interact with strangers, but as he
continued to press me in conversation about the Bible, it dawned on
me that I was being tested by God. Would I care for this non-Christian
whom God had sent to me? This was my ox that had fallen into a
ditch on the sabbath. God wanted to see what I would do.

I put aside my John manuscript and began sharing a heart-to-heart
with the man. I shared with him how Jesus' signs had been true in my
own life and how I was different because he was in my life. At first the
man seemed moved, but then he grew uninterested. He shared about
his Jewish heritage and some of his wounds from bad experiences with
Christians. His pain ran deep, and I knew that he needed something
more if he was going to become open to life in Jesus. So I prayed for God
to give me a word of knowledge to break through all of his defenses.

As we spoke, I tried to listen to the Holy Spirit for a divine word.
In my mind, I heard the name Barbara. I was going to act on what I
thought God had given to me.

I began by explaining, "This might sound a little weird, but I speak
to God and sometimes he speaks to me. I asked him if there was

something he wanted to say to you. I don't know for sure if this is from God, but can I share with you what I heard?"

"Sure, that's not weird. What did God say?" he replied matter-of-factly.

"I heard the name Barbara. Does that name mean anything to you?"

I envisioned that when the last syllable of her name rolled off my tongue, Borders would suddenly go into slow motion. I was prepared for him to throw his latte against the window, begin crying and start to pound the table as he shrieked, "Barbara is my mother. And I hate her!" (or something equally as dramatic).

Instead he stroked his graying beard, had a confused look on his face and said to me, "No, that name doesn't mean anything to me. But I appreciate you trying to be spiritual. I remember this one time I went to a palm reader. She looked at my palm and told me details there was no way she could know. Keep it up, buddy. Maybe in a couple of years you can be like her." And with that encouraging word, he picked up his coffee and left the table.

Soon after, I told Becky about my attempts to help the man at the bookstore experience Jesus. She laughed and laughed when I told her that palm readers were more spiritual than me. At least this failure brought color to our sabbath.

But was this really a failure? I believe that Jesus sent that man to me that day to examine what was in my heart. My personal vision for witness during that time was to try to develop the word of knowledge spiritual gift. God tested me to see if I really wanted him. Would I put aside my agenda, even my Bible study, to care for the man who was put before me? Would I be faithful to share the gospel with him? Would I risk looking dumb for the sake of trying to receive more of the Spirit whom God gives without measure? That day I didn't fail, though it sure looked and felt like I did. No, I was faithful with the little God had put before me. God tests his witnesses to take us to the next level.

When was the last time God tested your loyalty? Did you pass? Did you know you were being tested?

BEING PROACTIVE

Here are four areas where we can be proactive as we commit to becoming more passionate and effective witnesses.

Loving God's Word. As we seek to reach a culture that is ever more biblically illiterate, our love for God's Word will shine like a light in the darkness. As we see for ourselves the treasures found in God's Word, our lives will testify to the reliability of the Bible as an option for life. People at work and school will wonder what kind of treasure we have found when they see our passion and love for God's Word. We will have a sense of stability and peace and hope that they long for. But we must ourselves go deep with God to reach those treasures. We would do well to live out the resolution Jonathan Edwards made when he was twenty years old: "Resolved, to study the scriptures so steadily, constantly, and frequently, as that I may find, and plainly perceive myself to grow in the knowledge of the same."

In a day when lethargy and apathy are as common as cable TV, passion for God's Word will be a refreshing and stirring cry to the souls of our friends. As we deepen our experience with God's Word, we not only hasten our becoming more like Jesus, but we simultaneously equip ourselves with the single best tool for effective witness. As we devour more of the Word and make it the fabric of who we are, introducing people to Jesus will become second nature.

We must know the Word if we are to speak the Word. We must know the Word well to connect it to our daily lives and popular culture. This is contextualized evangelism—connecting God's Word to the already existing values of the people we are reaching.

I was spending the evening with a rap group at Cal State Dominguez Hills when the conversation shifted to professional wrestling. I seized the opportunity to tell them that Jesus was a spiritual wrestler. This startled them and got their attention. I then went on to tell the story, with intimate detail and passion, of the spiritual grudge match between Jesus and the devil in the wilderness. Suddenly Matthew 4 became more exciting for them than the pay-per-view wrestling event they had just watched. From my story, they saw an entirely new picture of Jesus and were therefore open to my invitation to my GIG. The Word became relevant and exciting to them. They wanted more and we started a GIG.

As we connect our friends to the Word, it becomes transformed for them from an irrelevant, antiquated book of rules into an exciting report of an amazing God. But if the Word of God is not in us, will we be able to convince them of their need for the Word? Without the Word ready to be delivered at any moment, we are left shaking our heads and nodding in agreement during the wrestling conversation. We miss our open door.

Mentors. Jesus walked with his disciples for three years, teaching them how to love God while on the earth. He trained them to be ministers. He showed them how to pray. He modeled for them what it looks like to do what the Father does. One of his greatest teaching agendas with the Twelve was witness.

In John 4 we read how Jesus mentored his followers in the dynamics of witness. From his interaction with the woman at the well, he taught them crosscultural, cross-gender, cross-class witness. When they saw her drop her water jar and give witness to her fellow villagers, they learned about the power of God's Word to transform lives. As the Samaritan villagers approached them, Jesus taught them about reaping, sowing and unexpected times for harvest. By the end of the experience, because of Jesus' mentoring in their lives, they were equipped (at least theoretically, until Jesus breathed on them) to lead citywide crosscultural revivals.

In the same way, you and I need active evangelism mentors. In his book *Connecting,* J. Robert Clinton defines mentoring as a relational experience through which one person empowers another by sharing God-given resources. We need witnesses who are more mature than us and who can teach us what God has taught them. Robert Coleman teaches us that one living sermon is worth a thousand explanations. How do fruitful evangelists prepare for and deliver their ministry? How do they build relationships? How do they keep their love fresh? We need to see it for ourselves.

Doug Schaupp, an IVCF staff worker in Los Angeles, has been my evangelism mentor off and on for the last ten years. God put him into my life the year I converted. I was immediately drawn to Doug and his bold, yet wise, style of witness. I closely observed how Doug shared his faith. I shadowed him whenever I could, taking notes on how he prayed, how he began conversations, how he spoke about Jesus and how he challenged people for commitment. I even noticed the look in his eye as he shared his faith. I memorized the Bible passages he taught so that I could teach them on my own. After a full season with Doug, I was off to become my own witness.

A couple of years ago, Doug invited me to partner with him to harvest non-Christians in a Bible study at a camp retreat. As we taught the Word together, I learned much by sitting under Doug's evangelism leadership. After each study, we would discuss our successes or failures, and he would teach me why he did what he did. Doug's proactive mentoring, though for only two dramatic seasons in my life, has made me the witness I am today.

We all need mentors. Especially in evangelism. They are out there; it's up to us to go get them.

Biographies. C. S. Lewis, in his book *Studies in Medieval and Renaissance Literature,* encourages us to read one "old" book—a work from a different generation—for every "new" book we read. It is a great charge. Reading old books will keep us honest and help us understand our generation against the backdrop of history. This exhortation is especially helpful for today's witnesses.

Bibliographies of the great witnesses in the history of the church often open doors that no current book can. When we read about passionate, single-minded, suffering soldiers of Christ, it strengthens the heart. The problems of today don't carry the same sting when we read about what our foremothers and forefathers went through for the sake of Jesus. During one season of my life and ministry, I was exhorted from beyond the grave as I read the testimony of all that David Brainerd, the great American missionary, went through as he lived sent by God. He never gave up—and he had it far worse than I did. Biographies will give us the perspective we need.

Boldness is redefined when we see how other saints lived their faith. Our often mild witness in current culture becomes woefully exposed when we see how much we embrace our current culture, which values harmony above all else. Spending regular time with witnesses of old will give us wisdom, passion and a fresh understanding of our own efforts to reach the world. The saints of old, through the written word, might just prove to be the best mentors God will ever give us.

Communication skills. When I was a student at UCLA, I was friends with Shon Tarver, the starting guard on the UCLA basketball team. He was a devout Christian and loved to share his faith. After graduation, he went on to play professional basketball in Japan. He also married his high school sweetheart. I met him for lunch shortly after his marriage and asked him what he liked best about married life. His answer caught me off-guard.

He said his favorite joy in being married was that he now had a practice partner for witness. They used their marriage to train one another to share their faith better. As they learned the new Japanese culture, they would create elaborate scenarios and role-play the different people they would meet on public transportation. They would practice what they would say to the Japanese non-Christians and then give each other feedback on their content, delivery, style and confidence. Shon's marriage made him a better witness.

We all need to become better communicators of the gospel. It needs to be a regular part of our lives. Are people captivated by our stories? If not, we have something to work on. Do we know how to effectively communicate the same key information in two-minute, five-minute and ten-minute slots? If not, we had better get to work. Do we know two or three Bible stories so well that we can use them to warm the souls of our non-Christian friends? That is a basic tool for today's witness. Have we learned to deliver persuasive and effective invitations to our GIGs so that people have the opportunity to become seekers? If we are faithful with little, we will become faithful with much.

Being used by God to rescue sinners is the highest call and demands our greatest attention. When we do not practice our communication skills and instead hope to "flow in the Spirit" or "be genuine and spontaneous," we are not loving the people we are sent to. I firmly believe that the Spirit of God will activate and anoint the words we speak, but if we have nothing to say, his anointing will never be experienced. Our friends deserve the best witness we can offer. If we are willing to develop calluses, we can become better communicators with our non-Christian friends.

GROWING CALLUSES

Joe Gevas, a senior at Cal State Dominguez Hills, is a great example of giving a full measure to become a faithful witness. Here is his testimony:

> When I entered the IVCF evangelism training this year, I knew I wanted to become an evangelist. I knew that in order to get closer to Jesus, I needed to take the next step and start witnessing to people. But I wasn't sure if I'd be able to. I was really self-

conscious about it, and I thought I had to learn the whole Bible front and back in order to be ready for people's questions during my GIGs. I did not feel confident enough. However, when I actually stepped out on a limb and started my first GIG, I realized that I didn't need to know everything and that God has my back no matter what, because I'm trying to teach his Word. I'm so glad that I challenged myself. It doesn't get easier, but I have learned, and I have developed to the next level. Sometimes I don't really feel like challenging myself, but afterward, I'm never left with regrets. I'm glad that GIGs push me to be a better teacher and a better servant.

The Word has shaped me as a witness this fall in a few different ways. My relationship with God has never been closer, and I keep improving it day by day. I've found that it's the little things that are important, like praying and reading the Bible every day and also writing in my journal (even though I still struggle with that). Making my relationship more solid with God enables me to share God with others better. Leading GIGs really makes me want to be a better Christian, one that walks the walk. Also, since I'm leading guys on my baseball team in GIGs, I can show them that I'm not perfect but that there is something different that distinguishes me from people who don't know Jesus. Studying the Word to teach others has really helped keep my relationship with Jesus that much closer. I'm really eager to keep pushing the envelope and keep serving God as a witness.

Jesus' work in me is seen most in my GIG with Mike. We had our last one of the semester this week, and it ended very strong. We went over Jesus' sixth sign from the Seven Signs GIG series. It was the healing of the blind beggar in John 9. I had been kind of worried about Mike. I thought he was losing interest and did not want to do the GIGs anymore. He kept ignoring my phone calls and would seem to always come up with an excuse. But I was persistent, and Jesus showed up in the last GIG. The first thing we did, which we haven't really been doing, was to ask questions. He hadn't really come up with any questions so far, so I asked him why. He said he had good questions, but he would forget them. So I gave him some examples of questions like "What is the difference between God and Jesus?" He really liked that question, and I answered it as best as I could. I then went on to explain the Bible in a nutshell to him. He also enjoyed that. Then we went on and did the GIG, which took kind of long but was interesting the whole time. It was especially good at the end when the Pharisees turned out to be the ones that were blind. I think he's really starting to see how Jesus works and the grace he has to give. When the GIG was over, he said, "This was the best GIG we've had so far."

Afterward, I challenged him and asked him what blocks he thought he had and how close he was to becoming a Christian. He said he's really far away. But I think he's closer than he thinks.

It was really a blessing to be able to lead my first GIG. I feel way more confident about leading GIGs now, and I realize that all I can do is show people who Jesus is. He will do the rest of the work. I've found the GIGs to be very humbling. Jesus works on his own time, not mine. I have to keep that in mind. All I can do is be a servant.

FINAL CHARGE FOR GROWTH

If we are not growing into more passionate, more confident, more powerful and more effective witnesses, we are not being faithful in the little God has given us. Will you become an outstanding witness? Are you willing to put in the time and hard work to develop the calluses? Bearing much fruit is not for the few born with the spiritual gift of evangelism; it is a promise for all of us. Please don't settle for witness blisters. Train yourself and grow by developing witness calluses.

BECOMING A GIG LEADER

At some point—breakthrough!
The momentum of the thing kicks in your favor,
hurling the flywheel forward, turn after turn . . .
whoosh! . . . its own heavy weight working for you.
You're pushing no harder than during the first rotation,
but the flywheel goes faster and faster.
Each turn of the flywheel builds upon work done earlier,
compounding your investment of effort.

JIM COLLINS

At this point, I trust you are excited to become a witness who gets the word out with more passion and effectiveness. In order to do that, we all need resources. In my own evangelism ministry I have found that GIGs (Groups Investigating God) are an excellent strategy for winning people to Jesus. GIGs have proven effective with college students, gang members, professionals, parents and grandparents. The Word of God proves able to penetrate Asian, white, Latino, African American, multiracial and all other cultures of the world. The Word of God contains eternal life and gives life to all people (John 6:63).

Becoming a fruitful GIG leader will take active faith and hard work. As God shapes you to become his witness, as you work on the disciplines of life in God to keep your faith alive, you will start to become that GIG leader. And you will experience what Jim Collins identifies as a turning point for great companies. Greatness does not come overnight; it comes over a lifetime. As you continue the uphill climb, moving forward with Jesus in witness day by day, then one day it will just seem to start going downhill. May you come to enjoy the fruit of your labors!

Following is a practical, step-by-step tool to assist you as you begin GIGs, your own Word-based personal evangelism ministry.

Please receive the same exhortation the apostle Paul gave to Timothy at Ephesus, encouraging him to lead strongly in his ministry of the Word. "Pay close attention to yourself and to your teaching; continue in these things, for in doing this you will save both yourself and your hearers" (1 Timothy 4:16).

INTRODUCTION TO GIGS

GIGs are small-group or one-on-one gatherings where Christians teach the Bible to their non-Christian friends. They are designed for non-Christians who would otherwise feel uncomfortable in a more formal religious context. The GIG creates a wonderful opportunity for Christians to take an active role of spiritual leadership and care in the lives of their friends.

If the discipleship programs of our Christian ministries are freeways with four lanes of cars whizzing by at seventy miles per hour, then GIGs are the on-ramp for non-Christians who are on the surface streets. They need an opportunity to join, at a pace that will allow them to merge without causing a ten-car pileup. How will they come to cruise at seventy miles per hour? How will they eventually find the joy of the carpool lane of discipleship? They must first enter onto the freeway. GIGs are great tools to help them convert while simultaneously preparing them for life in the Christian "fast lane."

Here are some reasons GIGs are the perfect on-ramp for our unchurched friends:

GIGs are a personal invitation. A GIG is attractive to the unchurched because it shows that we are serious about meeting their unique spiritual needs. GIGs are an invitation to our non-Christian friends to dine on spiritual food with us. GIGs help them feel cared for and heard in an age when Christians are perceived as being judgmental, narrow-minded and inflexible.

GIGs are about relationships. GIGs invite us to assert spiritual authority and leadership in the friendships with non-Christians God has already given us. It is the most natural destination for our friendships with non-Christians. Real friends share with one another their great triumphs and struggles with life. Jesus and the Word are part of every Christian's life. Where friendship already exists, GIGs build on the trust and love to help our friends experience the Source of love and relationships.

GIGs really are for the unchurched. Depending on our friends' background and level of hostility to Christianity, it is likely far more profitable for them to be involved in a GIG as opposed to a "Bible study." In a Bible study they will probably feel intimidated or not like the other people they are studying the Bible with. In the GIG, we don't subject our friends to Susie Christian sitting next to them glibly quoting the prophet Nahum. Nor do our friends feel the need to suddenly vomit when Joey Christian rambles on and on about some distant truth he has been spoon-fed for decades that has no relevant meaning for his life. GIGs keep it real and don't force our friends to embrace the culture of Christianity and miss Christ.

GIGs offer true spiritual experience. Our non-Christian friends are incurably spiritual. They look for spiritual experiences in music, movies and relationships. Why not lead them to the genuine spiritual experience of Jesus' Word? GIGs will connect people to the explosive power of the Bible. Our friends will not come to the conclusion that the Word is the best path for life on their own; they need a model and a guide. GIGs create that opportunity for us to lead them into the Bible.

God will win our friends. God will meet them and speak to them right where they are. We will be amazed at how the Holy Spirit will cause the words of Jesus to jump off the page and come alive in their daily experience. God will use the GIG to build trust with our friends and prove to them that following him is the best investment of their life.

GIGs offer discipleship foundations. GIGs will give our biblically illiterate friends an excellent base upon which to begin their life of discipleship. Their time in the GIG will deepen them in the Word. They will understand the teachings of Jesus and what it means to follow him through what we teach them in the GIGs. When they are ready to commit to Jesus and follow him, they will know what they are committing to. As Jesus increases his calls for more of their life, they won't be surprised as if something has suddenly been switched on them. Great GIGs lead to great converts.

TRUST

Leading GIGs is an intentional choice. Becoming a vessel of God's water that satisfies the spiritual thirst of others will not just happen. It is an intentional choice to love. Putting others in our day planner to meet with them does not make them a project. It means that we care enough about them to block out our time and make sure we don't stand them up.

I am aware that there are real temptations in being intentional. None of us is pure in heart. We must fight hard to keep our motives in check. But if we choose not to be intentional in our love, the battle to make disciples through GIGs has already been lost.

It is important that our friends trust us. When they trust us, we will be able to use our friendship to help awaken curiosity about Christ. Some folks will immediately trust us and feel right at home with our becoming their spiritual mentors. These folks will likely join our GIGs right away.

Others, however, might not trust us right away. We might be walking into the pain of experiences they have previously had with church or other Christians. Some of these wounds may not be healed. For these folks, it is crucial to help them ease into our GIG. It would be wise to help them experience the servant love of Jesus (John 13:1-17). They may initially feel hostile or apathetic, but we can know that God is using us to break his light into their life. We should be patient with them, for God is usually doing more in them than they let on.

Do what they do. Our friends don't care how much we know until they know how much we care. It is crucial that we get to know them! Dave Palmer, who led me to Jesus, built trust with me by talking hoops and shooting baskets with me. He did that intentionally because he knew I loved ball. He got onto the basketball court with me before inviting me into his Bible study. That sure helped me be open to his invitation to join his GIG.

What hobbies are your friends into? What music do they listen to? Do what they do (drawing the line at sin, of course).

Serve them. We can build trust as we care for others by meeting practical needs. Supplying them with food, treating them to evenings of entertainment and caring for them when they are sick—these are just a few of the basic acts of service I have seen God bless. This is especially true in the urban ministry context. We will gain a voice when we show that we understand the problems and are part of the solution. In the city context, word without deed erodes trust. When our friends ask us why we are so nice or comment on how we are different from other Christians, that is a sign that real trust is happening.

In regard to trust, our friends do not need to be our *best* friends to come to our GIG. Many of us have far more trust with our friends than we realize, yet we don't cash in on it to help them grow closer to God. Our friends already trust us. We just need to show them Jesus.

CURIOSITY AND THE INVITATION

Here are some of the best ways I have seen to build trust and help non-Christians become curious about Jesus:

Be full of passion and integrity. I listened to Dave and his invitation to me because Dave lived as if God were real. I knew God existed because Dave lived like he did. He lived Jesus' words to the point of cleaning our entire dorm floor after a shaving cream fight at 4:00 in the morning. With each scrub on his hands and knees, Dave's God became more real. Passion and integrity speak more clearly in the trust-building stage than anything one can speak. As Becky Pippert writes in *Out of the Saltshaker*, the first Bible people will read is our life.

Have fun. Many of our non-Christian friends have perceptions that Christians are so religious and so stuffy that we don't enjoy having fun. Nothing could or should be further from the truth.

During lunch one weekend in my UCLA dorm, my friend Jason shared with us that if we gave him $100 we could shave his head any way we wanted. From those around the table we collected $90. We scoured the dorm floor and realized the only person left who hadn't gone home for the weekend was Dave, the Bible study leader. I assumed he wouldn't be interested in the shaving of Jason's head because he was religious. But with no other choice, I asked Dave if he wanted in on shaving Jason's head. He jumped up from his computer, got $10 and said he would be in if he could do some of the shaving. It was a great moment. By joining our afternoon project of head shaving, Dave shattered stereotypes and became more real to me. We ended up giving Jason a Bozo-the-Clown shave, leaving hair only on the side of his head. It was great.

Have fun with your friends!

Speak relevant language. Jesus spoke in parables so that the common people could understand his message. Similarly, our language must be reinvented if we are going to communicate with our postmodern non-Christian friends. They need us to be the Christian-to-non-Christian dictionary for them. Why tell them we are going to Bible study, accountability prayertime and a harvest conference when they have no idea what that means? Speaking relevant language is hard work. Are you willing to be intentional and reinvent your vocabulary for the sake of your friends?

Be vulnerable. We all have real problems and real joys in our life, so let's grow in learning how to bring our non-Christian friends into the middle of our emotional life. One of the most effective ways of building trust for me this year has been sharing about my own insecurities and struggles. In sharing vulnerably about my life, I become real to people. What would happen if all of us shared about our joys, our fears, our bad days, our good days and our struggles with our parents? Our friends need to know we are real people and not Christian robots.

The invite. The challenge of witness will increase when it is time for us to open our mouth and invite our friends to our GIG. As we think about inviting them to our GIG, it is easy to get all worked up about what they might think. *Am I pressuring them? Am I jeopardizing the friendship? Am I being ungenuine?* The truth, however, is that they probably aren't thinking about those issues at all. I have found that if they do feel those things, they will tell me. I also ask them regularly if I am coming on too strong. They appreciate a question like that.

I challenge you to assume that they will be open to your invitation. Think about why the GIG will be good for them. A generic invitation does not show that you have thought about your friends and care for them. Deliver your invite with confidence. The smoother you are, the smoother it will be for them.

Here are some tips you might consider to help you construct a compelling and confident invite:

- Tell them your GIG is a spiritual discussion for people who don't identify with church. (This is not always effective with African American people, who often hold church in high regard.)

- Tell them it is a chance to learn in a friendly environment.

- Tell them why you think they would like Jesus.

- Tell them that it is only an hour (and don't go long).

Our non-Christian friends are far more eager for, and open to, our spiritual leadership than we think.

CHALLENGING AND TEACHING OUR FRIENDS

Preparing to teach. As your friends have committed to your GIG (place and time), you are now ready to unleash Jesus' Word into their lives. As you prepare to teach, here are some tips to help you develop into a strong teacher of God's Word.

- Pray that God will increase your spiritual authority to teach his Word.

- Personally invest yourself—love the Bible for yourself.

- Pick passages from the Word that will appeal to your friends.

- Pick passages that highlight Jesus' life and reveal why he is unique.

- Teach from passages that have changed your own life.

- Work hard to understand the passage beforehand and arrive prepared.

- Write out questions that flesh out the main points of the text.

- Have a long-term perspective and know that becoming a great teacher takes years.

For information on GIG series resources that I have developed, visit the Get the Word Out Ministries website: <www.gtwoministries.com>.

Setting the rules. As the GIG leader, you will find that setting some rules goes a long way toward establishing a learning environment. The worst GIGs are those that spin out of control because a few don't want to learn and eventually ruin it for those who genuinely want to grow. Rules prevent such problems.

At the first GIG of a new series, I always teach the rules for the GIG. My friends don't feel burdened by the rules; they actually like them because it helps them learn. Here are the four rules I present as I begin to lead a GIG:

1. Be open to growing spiritually and applying what you learn.

2. Choose to be curious and ask your questions.

3. Answer our questions from the text.

4. Be cool with each other and treat each other with respect.

Teaching the text. As I teach Scripture to my friends, I try to hold a balance between being a facilitator and being a leader. I encourage initiative and challenge the others to interact with the text on their own, and then I fan the flames of their discussion. Seeing treasure in the Word for oneself can be a life-changing experience.

At the same time, however, I know they come to the GIG to be taught. They have voted for my leadership by showing up. I care enough about their experience to make sure they don't leave feeling the GIG was a waste of time.

Don't be afraid to teach during the GIG. You are the leader; sometimes you facilitate and sometimes you lead strongly. Your friends are there looking for leadership. Don't let them leave wishing you would have stepped up.

Making it real—application. The most important part of the GIG is application. As our friends spend time in the Word, Jesus will reveal himself to them. They will see his character, his wisdom, his glory and his love. They will likely comment that Jesus is different from what they thought he was like. But if it ended there, the GIG experience would be largely academic. For true change, however, our friends must *experience* the good news, not only hear it.

It is crucial that we have a genuine testimony for how the Word has been true for us. Our friends need to know that Jesus is real, and they will see his reality in our life. Sharing is the currency of our culture, and we need to speak the language of the culture.

As you prepare to teach the Word, ask yourself questions about how Jesus has been real to you from the passage. How has he touched you and brought healing? How has he taught you? How has he answered your questions and resolved your doubts? If you don't have stories from your own life, find stories from friends, Christian biographies or anywhere else the GIG members can see Jesus' goodness in action.

I end the sharing time by assuring the GIG participants that if God did it for me, he will do it for them. I prepare a question that will cause them to go to Jesus and invite him to break into their lives. I tell them that going to Jesus, inviting him to act, is how to have faith. If I didn't have a well-prepared story of God's reality to share with them, they would leave with only a Bible study. GIGs can be way more than an exercise in amassing spiritual knowledge. Make it real for your folks!

Index cards. I end the GIG by passing out index cards. I ask my friends to write down one question they have about God and one issue they are currently grappling with in their lives. I inform them that I want to pray for them and answer any questions they might have. I then try to start the next GIG by answering one of their questions about the kingdom.

I am constantly amazed at what my friends are going through and the freedom they feel to tell me their issues. Here are some of the questions and comments I have received on index cards:

• "How can you prove the Bible is true? Why should I have faith?"

- "Does God love me after what I have done? Am I kidding myself?"

- "Why is God so vengeful?"

- "Why do I feel like God is not there when I need him most?"

- "Are heaven and hell real? I want to go to heaven. How do I get there?"

- "What do I do if I can't forgive myself for all the terrible things I have done?"

- "I need God to help me with my drinking problem."

- "My friends keep letting me down because they are selfish. What do I do?"

The cards serve two main functions in the GIGs. First, the cards offer a great opportunity to know what legitimate questions people are thinking about so that we can pick passages and help their process of becoming disciples. Second, the cards create a chance to help our friends with their deepest problems. As they share their pain, we can lead them to the Jesus who touches our deepest levels of pain and brokenness.

The fullness of grace and truth. As you lead your GIG and pick passages for your people, make sure they are challenged by Jesus' Word. Show them the Jesus who touched and healed the lepers as well as the Jesus who commanded his people to hate their sin and carry their cross.

A couple of years ago, I made the error of focusing too heavily on the grace of God. After six studies, my friends thought Jesus was great but had no desire to follow him. His grace was like the flavor-of-the-month to them. They needed to know that Jesus gives grace but that he also swings truth. So at the next GIG, I taught them Jesus' parable on the ten maidens from Matthew 25. Jesus had no problem affirming the wise women who were ready for the party while calling the ones who weren't prepared fools!

As we began our study, Brett started shifting in his seat, obviously feeling uncomfortable. He stopped the study during observations and blared out, "What happened to Jesus?"

I asked him what he meant.

Then Brett asked, "Where is the grace?"

I asked him what new truths he had picked up about Jesus.

He then said soberly, "I can't #*$% around with Jesus!"

In being overly focused on encouraging people and eager to show them Jesus' grace, we keep them from Jesus the leader. It might well be his strong calls that open the hearts of our friends. It is his grace to call people to the hard truths of the kingdom. Our non-Christian friends will respect Jesus more when they hear the whole gospel. People who are open to change want to be challenged. They are tired of leaders who only bring comfort. They will be drawn to a Jesus who brings change.

Giving a challenge. Our friends need to be challenged to become genuine seekers. This is an important step in the process of conversion. If we do not challenge our friends, it is likely they will never enter the kingdom of God.

Jesus was ruthless in discerning people's hearts and speaking truth to them. How else can one describe him when he shamed Nicodemus, Israel's teacher, who didn't know the truth about the regeneration of the heart (John 3:10)? We see this love that went beyond nice chatter when Jesus asked the lame man at the pool if he wanted to be well. We see it again when Jesus proclaimed that the religious leaders would die in their sins unless they turned and came to him (John 8:24). Jesus never held back truth. He spoke with clarity, authority and power. His words were challenging and made people think when they left him. Jesus knew that strong challenges are loving acts for a potential seeker.

The conversation. Have you ever had "the conversation" with a non-Christian? The symptoms of such a conversation are queasiness in the stomach, sweaty palms and fervent prayer. The fears of such a conversation are that you will be put into the same camp with the intolerant, offensive Christians whom your friends have told you they hate so much.

But in his love for our non-Christian friends, God will lead us into conversations where we will challenge our friends to live differently. There are no shortcuts to faith. Like everyone else, they must go through the narrow door that leads to life.

My friend Scott was seemingly open to Jesus. We were wonderful friends and did everything together. He came to my Bible study and told me how much he respected my life of faith. But he didn't want to change his life to follow Jesus. His block was having sex with many different women. I knew God wanted me to help him, so one evening I invited him over to my apartment for dinner. I told him that I needed to have a heart-to-heart with him.

I laid out the patterns that I saw in his life and asked him if he also saw those themes. He said he did. I then passionately explained Jesus' offer of healing and told him that satisfaction—true satisfaction—awaited him if he chose Jesus. He said he appreciated my thinking about him, but he wanted to do his own thing.

I then went to another level and told him that as he turned his back on God, eternal punishment was a real option for him. I told him I loved him and didn't want him to spend forever in hell. He reiterated that he just wasn't "feeling" Jesus. My heart fell.

I feel that I have done right by Scott. The blood is not on my hands. God sent me to become a well for a thirsty man, and I did my best. It is now on Scott in terms of how he handles the treasure of the gospel.

I still have hope for Scott. Today we are still friends. He came to celebrate with me at my wedding. I still pray that God will use the challenge to open Scott's heart. He has heard the truth.

Have you had "the conversation"? If not, prepare yourself, because you will. That is how much Jesus loves your friends in your GIG!

SEEKERS

Once our friends are open to change and become seekers, conversion is almost inevitable. If they have truly opened their heart to change, Jesus has a wonderful opening to move in with his grace. Yet sometimes we approach conversion as though it were a difficult golf putt. We put unnecessary pressure on ourselves because we think we need to hit the perfect fifty-foot shot on undulating greens for our friend to become a Christian. But leading our friends through the process of becoming a genuine seeker is more like a miniature golf shot. We don't need the touch of Tiger Woods, because we are hitting the ball into a giant funnel that will spit it out right into the hole. Once our friends are actively seeking Jesus, commitment becomes a viable next step.

The inherent weakness in the GIG model of witness is helping people become full disciples in a worshiping community. For the person who comes from a nonreligious background, embracing a Christian community can be a great challenge. Here are some steps we might take to prevent new believers from never joining the body that can help ensure their spiritual development and growth:

- Pray that they become committed to the Christian community.

- At the beginning of the GIG, teach them that Jesus is all about team and community.

- Help them build trust in the larger community of faith.

- After their conversion, have them give public testimony of their faith to the new community.

- Once they convert, help them see themselves as leaders.

- Stress the role of Bible study in community.

- Be quick to ask them about how their transition is going.

- Develop in them the habit of regular church attendance.

BECOMING NEW DISCIPLES

Here are some thoughts on how to lead people to become disciples of Jesus:

- Review how you have seen God at work in the lives of your friends.

- Help them understand that Jesus wants long-term commitment.

- Take a deep breath, look them in the eye and invite them to follow Christ.

- Feel free to persuade them. Help them see what a great decision this is.

- Give them a new-believer growth plan to ensure they begin healthy discipleship.

CLOSING BLESSING

Breakthrough comes almost unnoticeably for those who are committed to growth. As we get the word out and lead GIGs, God will increase our vision and our zeal for the lost. May we experience more breakthrough in our personal evangelism ministry than we ever imagined possible. The word that God has put inside of us must get out. Getting the word out and seeing it give life to our friends is one of purest joys in this world. May you, your friends and your family know that joy! Peace.

ACKNOWLEDGMENTS

This book is the product of a community. As I write, I am guided by those who have invested in me. God has been good to give me wonderful family, friends, partners and mentors. As you read this book, if you find anything that encourages you, increases your faith, or grows your hope for the world, the following people are most likely responsible for that grace.

I fear to think where I would be today if not for my mother, Yung Soon Whang Teter. Her unusual strength, pioneering spirit and inexhaustible love are the pillars of my life. She has taught me much, and if not for her, I would certainly have made shipwreck of my life. I thank her for believing in me and hoping for me, through good times and bad. She is one of my few heroes in this world.

I thank God for Francis Fillerup, George and Andrew Teter. It is a gift to have family like you.

I am thankful to God for David Palmer. Ten years ago he brought me to Christ, and today he leads me deeper into Christ with his passion for Scripture and his enduring zeal as a missionary. His life is a testimony to the joy God sets before us.

My love and respect for Doug Schaupp only grow with the years. He was my staff worker in college, and he skillfully taught me how to live in Jesus' kingdom. Ten years later I appreciate all the more what he has given me. He is a true and faithful friend.

Alex Gee and I met by "accident" in 1996. Today I see God's grace and wisdom in bringing us together. Alex's love, wisdom and humor help me experience the goodness and greatness of God.

I am blessed with a wonderful InterVarsity Christian Fellowship staff team for the work at Dominguez Hills and Compton College. Mailin Chu, Vikki Leung, Eddie Gonzales and Edgar Esqueda are great missionaries and even better friends. I honor April Hanson, Stephanie Easton and Norlyn Palaam for their tremendous contributions to More Than Conquerors. And it has been amazing leading and learning urban ministry with Brad Arnold.

I thank the More Than Conquerors students at Dominguez Hills and Compton. I am so proud of all of you. Thank you for giving Becky and me so much life. We love you.

I have been shaped by God through key mentors he has put in my life. What grace to be developed by such outstanding people as Alex Van Riesen, Sandy Schaupp, Enrique Santis, Darrell Johnson, Shelley Trebesch and Bobby Clinton. Jesus said that whoever teaches others to keep his words will be called great in the kingdom (Matthew 5:19). You are all great.

I am so honored to work with passionate, wonderful leaders in IVCF. Thanks to Alec Hill, Rich Lamb, Terry Erickson, Rick Richardson, Judy Johnson, Steve Stuckey, Susie Veon and Doug Ribbens. These folks make it great to be an evangelist in IVCF.

Cindy Bunch and Andy Le Peau at InterVarsity Press have been a great blessing to me. They went out of their way to give a new author a chance to write. I am thankful for their support, their wisdom and their encouragement.

I give special thanks and honor to my ministry support team. Without them, Becky and I would not be experiencing the kingdom dreams God has put into our souls. I highlight the sacrificial partnership and ministry of Jeff Hanson, John Tumminello, Brian Ingkom, Jon Recker, the Reckers in Seattle, Sharon Ruckman, Joe and Angie Lynch, Tom and Diane Schull, Mary Huey, Agape Fellowship at

Glendale Presbyterian Church, Julie Chan, Joshua Griffin and my brother under the purple and gold banners, Isaac Flores. These partners are simply the best.

Carol, Tim, Caroline and Debbie Sato have been amazing during the course of this project. Their love, laughs and flexibility have encouraged me immeasurably. Tim is a great editor with sharp, clear ideas. His assistance has lifted this project more than a few dramatic notches.

I honor my father-in-law, George Kiyoshi Sato, who entered the kingdom of God this past year. Evangelism was his passion, and for over forty years he labored for and won the lost in this dark world. He was a burning, shining lamp who now shines with the other great saints in Jesus' presence. I thank him for the life of passionate evangelism he modeled for us. We miss him dearly.

And most important, I thank and honor my wife, Becky, to whom this book is dedicated. I respect her immensely, love her deeply and look forward to growing old with her. She is my treasure and joy on this earth.

CONTACT INFORMATION

To contact John Teter, you can e-mail him at gettthewordout@charter.net

To learn more about the InterVarsity Christian Fellowship campus work in Long Beach, California, check out the website for More Than Conquerors: <www.ivcfmetrosouth.org >.

To find out more about John Teter's evangelism ministries and resources, visit Get the Word Out Ministries: <www.gtwoministries.com >.